EN

David Oh has done an outstanding job removing the sometimes mystical undertone to the prophetic and presenting it in a very clear, concise and easy to follow layout. This book is filled with solid sound biblical teaching as well as real life examples on the practical application of prophesy. It is with great pleasure that I recommend Beginning in the Prophetic for everyone who has a desire to hear God's voice and partner with Him in calling forth His purposes into existence.

Dr. Ché Ahn
Senior Pastor, HROCK Church
President, Harvest International Ministry
International Chancellor, Wagner Leadership Institute
Pasadena, CA

I highly recommend reading Beginning in the Prophetic as a great how-to manual for hearing God. David answers many questions that we all have as we begin listening to the voice of God and steers us in the right direction as we journey deeper into the prophetic.

Cheryl Allen
Director, Pasadena International House of Prayer
Pasadena, CA

This is a powerful, easy to read, practical book on the gift of prophecy. It will open up a whole new dimension of the Christian life for those who have not walked in this gift, and it will greatly strengthen the prophetic ministry of those who do.

David Oh is a 'Revelatory' teacher who releases the Spirit of Revelation as he shares. This whole book is good, but his teachings on the difference between Old and New Covenant prophecy is worth the price of the book alone. And, as you read about his own journey into the prophetic, you will find your hope rising to believe that you too can change lives and history through the gift of prophecy. I highly recommend this book.

STEVE BACKLUND
Global Legacy/BSSM Leadership Deployment, Bethel Church
Ignited Hope Ministries
Redding, CA

Beginning in the Prophetic shows the reader practical steps on how to hear from God, because once you've asked Him to speak to you, He will. Our job is to figure out the way He is speaking to us. David helps us find the Lord rather than formulas and tips to improve in the prophetic. David shares the heart of the Father wanting a more intimate connection with His children.

THOMAS BLACKMON
Healing Rooms Team Leader, Bethel Church
Redding, CA

David not only clarifies the prophetic, his explanations and examples are clear, understandable, practical and doable. For the individual pursuing the prophetic this is a must read. You will receive an impartation of the prophetic, and as an additional bonus, the supernatural as you traverse this book. This is an easy read.

LES COOMBS
Healing Rooms Pastor, Bethel Church,
Redding, CA

Beginning in the Prophetic is a refreshingly practical and empowering resource to grow in one of the most life-giving, essential gifts the Lord has given to the body of Christ. It is uniquely comprehensive—David provides a biblical foundation and value for the prophetic as well as current examples and illustrations of prophecy. He addresses common questions and barriers to the prophetic, offers down to earth instruction and application of how to grow in it, recognizes and encourages diverse expressions of prophecy, and also gives helpful insight about receiving from and stewarding the prophetic. David has created an introduction to the prophetic that feels safe and accessible for anyone. And perhaps most importantly, he identifies the heart and spirit behind the prophetic is love, honor and relationship. The prophetic is a gift the Lord has made available to us, but ultimately it is something that cultivates the greatest gift of all—a love relationship with Him. You will be encouraged, empowered, blessed and activated as you read—enjoy!

KATE EIFERT
Revival Pastor in BSSM, Bethel Church
Redding, CA

David lives out an intimate connection with the Lord experiencing and releasing a prophetic lifestyle. With his advanced theological training, he has put together this book on the prophetic to also be true to the word of God. I so appreciate David's heart for the body of Christ and his desire to train and activate its newest members into seeing, believing, and speaking the word of the Lord. This book is designed for beginners to get a clear and comprehensive view of the prophetic, which has been often misunderstood. This man has a gifted, multifaceted ministry to the body, including healing. And although this may be his first writing effort, I'm sure it is just the beginning of many. This book should be read by everyone with a peaked interest in the prophetic ministry.

KARL MALOUFF
Executive Pastor, HROCK Church
Pasadena, CA

David Oh, with skillful use of wisdom and Scripture, guides us into the heart of theprophetic. David's approach demystifies the gift of prophecy and the culture that surrounds it. "Beginning in the Prophetic" illuminates the governing dynamics and underlying principles surrounding the gift of prophecy. This book endeavors to serve as a manual for experiencing the true essence of the prophetic. It gracefully draws readers towards excellence in hearing God's voice while giving a sense of security. David passionately coaches the reader with the nuts and bolts of the prophetic and the simplistic beauty of prophetic expression. I enthusiastically recommend this book to anyone desiring to hear God's voice.

AJAY SAMUEL
Prophetic Director, Pasadena International House of Prayer
Pasadena, CA

It is rare to find an author who is able to introduce a multi-faceted subject in a brief, concise, and thoroughly readable manner without sacrificing clarity or skimping on the essentials. David Oh has produced delightful evidence of just this kind of skill and gifting in the pages of Beginning in the Prophetic. I heartily recommend this prophetic primer, not only to those taking their first steps in prophetic ministry, but also to seasoned prophets who are often called upon to help de-mystify this gift for the equipping and encouragement of the saints. Allow David to "open the door" to the vast treasure room of prophetic ministry and you'll find your appetite whet for more of God's communication to and through his children.

STEVE TRULLINGER
Founding Servant, The Father's Touch Ministries
Chancellor, Wagner Leadership Institute – South Bay
Torrance, California

BEGINNING IN THE PROPHETIC

LEARNING HOW TO SAY WHAT THE FATHER IS SAYING

BURNING LAMP™
media & publishing

BEGINNING IN THE PROPHETIC by David Oh
Published by BURNING LAMP MEDIA & PUBLISHING
An Imprint of DOMINION LEADERSHIP SOLUTIONS

P.O. Box 1284
Haymarket, VA 20168
www.burninglampmap.com

ISBN-10: 1937481042
ISBN-13: 978-1937481049

Cover Design: Anthony Antenucci of Zakr Studios
Interior Design: Gabriel Leonhard of Voyage Media Group

Printed in the United States of America
First Edition 2012

DEDICATION

This book is dedicated to my wife and children. I declare you will see what the prophets of old longed to see and help an entire generation experience their prophetic destiny. I love you more than words can express.

ACKNOWLEDGMENTS

As with most significant endeavors in our lives, there are numerous individuals who help us through the process. Thank you to all my editors (Anna, Sally, and Tiffany), Brian Francis Hume and Burning Lamp Publishing, Pastor Min, Steve Trullinger, and everyone who has ever prophesied over me. I would also like to thank…

My parents and relatives for their continued support

My brother and his family for believing in me

My mother and father-in-law for their prodigal love

Everyone at Bethel Church for demonstrating what a healthy prophetic culture looks like and prophesying destiny I didn't even know I had

The HRock and PIHOP communities for welcoming us into the family

Isaac, Abigail, and Anna for teaching me about grace, freedom, and the joy of the Father

My wife, Jenney, for making me whole and being my everything

And the Holy Spirit, Jesus, and Father God for helping the impossible become possible

ABOUT DAVID

David and his wife Jenney currently live in Pasadena, CA with their three children Isaac, Abigail, and Anna. They enjoy doing life together with the Pasadena International House of Prayer and HRock Church family.

CONTENTS

BEGINNING IN THE PROPHETIC

LEARNING HOW TO SAY WHAT THE FATHER IS SAYING

INTRODUCTION

In 2009, the Lord spoke to me very clearly; he told me that I was going to write a book. I started laughing. In school, English had been one of my least favorite subjects. Writing papers and essays was a painful experience. How could I write an entire book? Unsure of what to do or even how to begin, I went on with my life as usual.

Just a few weeks later, a Christian I had never met before prophesied over me, saying God had given me a revelatory writing gift. I blurted out, "What did you say?"

He repeated the word and proceeded to tell me I had a special grace to write like a particular author. He told me the name of the author, not knowing that this person was actually one of my favorite writers!

Several months later, I was ministering at a conference in Ecuador when a believer from Brazil gave me a piece of paper with a picture on it. It was a book with the words "Beginning Prophetic" on the front. I didn't know what it meant until he later told me that I was going to write a book about prophetic ministry.

Since that time, I have committed to being faithful with what the Lord has told me and have been devoting a significant portion of my time to writing. This book is the firstfruit of that prophetic word, and I know it is only the start of much more. *Beginning in the Prophetic* introduces the prophetic ministry to those who have had limited or no experience with the gift of prophecy. My prayer is that you will encounter the Holy Spirit in these pages and open your eyes to the importance of prophecy. May you eagerly desire the prophetic gift and receive it with gladness.

I declare that you are part of a prophetic generation of believers who will boldly say what the Father is saying to those who desperately long to hear from God!

CHAPTER 1
What is Prophecy?

"Follow the way of love and eagerly desire spiritual gifts, especially the gift of prophecy." (NIV 1984)

"Pursue love, yet desire earnestly spiritual gifts, but especially that you may prophesy." (NASB)

"Let love be your highest goal! But you should also desire the special abilities the Spirit gives—especially the ability to prophesy." (NLT)

—1 Corinthians 14:1

The Apostle Paul makes a clear and intriguing statement. On the heels of his classic passage on love, he writes, "Follow the way of love and eagerly desire gifts of the Spirit, *especially prophecy*" (1 Corinthians 14:1; emphasis added) . Out of all the gifts of the Spirit Paul mentions in his letter to the church in Corinth, he highlights prophecy as the gift that should be highly sought. Although the gifts of wisdom, knowledge, faith, tongues and its interpretation, discerning of spirits, healings, and even miracles are amazing graces given to the church, prophecy is something all believers are to covet. What is it about prophecy that prompted Paul to issue a command and not a suggestion for its acquisition? Let us begin answering that by defining prophecy.

Prophecy defined

Prophecy is communicating what the Father is saying in a way that strengthens, encourages, or comforts others. Paul described prophecy as a grace or gift of the Holy Spirit meant for the common good, not solely for the individual:

> Now to each one the manifestation of the Spirit is given for the common good. To one there is given through the Spirit . . . prophecy . . . All these are the work of one and the same Spirit, and he gives them to each one, just as he determines.
>
> —1 Corinthians 12:7-11

According to Steve Thompson, "Prophecy includes the spiritual gifts of *a word of knowledge, word of wisdom, discerning of spirits, and the gift of prophecy*" (emphasis added)[1]. I will provide a brief description of the first three, but the main focus of this book will be on the gift of prophecy.

Word of knowledge

Prophecy is communicating what the Father is saying in a way that strengthens, encourages, or comforts others.

A word of knowledge is information the Holy Spirit gives an individual that he did not know previously—information that is usually about another person. Jesus received a word of knowledge when he conversed with a Samaritan woman at a well in John 4. He told her to get her husband and come back. She replied that she didn't have a husband. Jesus said to her,

> You are right when you say you have no husband. The fact is, you have had five husbands, and the man you now have is not your husband. What you have just said is quite true." She immediately responded, "Sir, I can see that you are a prophet.
>
> —John 4:17-19

Jesus knew this information, not through a town gossip,

1 Steve Thompson, You May All Prophesy, (US: MorningStar Publications, Inc.; 2007), 11

but by the word of knowledge gift. The woman did not reveal any of her background to Jesus. The Holy Spirit gave this information to Jesus so that the Samaritan woman could experience the power of God and embrace the truth. This gift demonstrated the heart of the Father because through this woman's encounter many people from her town came to believe in Jesus as the Savior of the world.[2]

Words of knowledge can also occur in the context of healing. I was having lunch at a restaurant with a friend, when the owner came out to talk with us. As she was speaking, I asked God if she needed prayer for anything. God highlighted the back of her shoulder. During a break in the conversation, I inquired if she had any pain or problems with her shoulder and pointed to the specific area on my own shoulder. She exclaimed, "You have no idea!" and then told us how she had recently fallen on the exact spot I had pointed to and was experiencing severe pain. She then allowed my friend and me to pray for her shoulder, and all of her pain instantly went away!

Word of wisdom

The gift of the word of wisdom is the skillful application of knowledge. It is a divine grace to know the right thing to do at the right time. A word of wisdom is often directional in nature because it contains prophetic insight about what should be done in a particular situation. This gift may also entail the revealing of prophetic destiny—speaking hidden

2 John 4:39-42

truths of what is not known.[3]

God offered King Solomon anything he wanted, and Solomon asked for an understanding heart so he could rule the people with wisdom. God was so moved by Solomon's response that He granted his request and added riches and honor to it.[4]

In the very next passage, Solomon demonstrated his wisdom when two prostitutes came before him arguing over who was the rightful mother of a baby. Solomon cleverly declared the baby should be cut in two and that half be given to each woman. Through his proclamation, he discovered the true mother to be the woman unwilling to see her child killed. "When all Israel heard the verdict the king had given, they held the king in awe, because they saw that he had wisdom from God to administer justice" (1 Kings 3:28). The Father's heart of truth and justice was revealed through a spiritual gift.

Discerning of spirits

The gift of discerning of spirits is the ability to determine which spirit is guiding a person. The existence of this gift implies there are different types of spirits which operate in people's lives. Just as believers listen to and follow the Holy Spirit, everyone can be influenced by other spirits—whether we realize it or not. The three main types of spirits people can listen to are the Holy Spirit, their own spirits, or evil spirits.

A sorcerer and false prophet named Bar-Jesus (also called

3 cf. Corinthians 2:6-16
4 1 Kings 3

Elymas) lived on the island of Cyprus. Elymas was obviously being led by an evil spirit. He opposed Barnabas and Saul and tried to turn others from the faith.

> Those who prophesy are kingdom ambassadors who make a way for individuals to draw closer to the Lord.

Saul, who was also called Paul, was filled with the Holy Spirit. He looked straight at Elymas and said, "You are a child of the devil and an enemy of everything that is right! You are full of all kinds of deceit and trickery. Will you never stop perverting the right ways of the Lord?" (Acts 13:10). Paul used the gift of discerning of spirits to judge that Bar-Jesus was a false prophet who wasn't listening to the Holy Spirit but rather evil spirits.

The gift of prophecy

Prophecy is simply "hearing" from God and lovingly expressing to others what you hear for their blessing.[5] Hearing is in quotations because communication from the Lord comes in various forms, many of which are not physically audible. Although people have differing experiences, understandings, and even theories about it, prophecy is a gift of the Holy Spirit meant to build up the church and promote love.

The Apostle Paul clearly states everyone who prophesies speaks to people for their strengthening, encouragement,

5 See chapter 4 "Hearing From God"

and comfort. *The Message* translation puts it this way: "But when you proclaim his truth in everyday speech [prophesy], you're letting others in on the truth so that they can grow and be strong and *experience his presence with you*" (1 Corinthians 14:3, emphasis added). Prophetic words can lead people into an encounter with God's presence. Prophecy is a divine invitation for fellowship and intimacy. Those who prophesy are kingdom ambassadors who make a way for individuals to draw closer to the Lord.

Foretelling and forth-telling

Prophecy is typically delivered in the form of either foretelling or forth-telling. Foretelling is the act of predicting or declaring the future. Forth-telling is calling things into being.

Foretelling

Foretelling seems to be the predominant method of prophecy in the Bible. It also tends to be the more common understanding of prophecy among people today. The Spirit of God is eternal and knows how all things will unfold. The Lord chooses to reveal certain future events so people will be better informed and prepared for the magnitude of an occasion. For example, in Acts 11:27-28 Agabus foretold a severe famine, and when he did, the disciples decided to take up an offering for the church in Judea: "During this time some prophets came down from Jerusalem to Antioch. One of them, named Agabus, stood up and through the Spirit predicted that a severe famine would spread over the entire Roman world.

(This happened during the reign of Claudius.)"

Perhaps the most important prophecies in the Old Testament were the words given about the Christ. Ever since the fall of humanity in the Garden of Eden, all of creation has been in need of a Savior to bring reconciliation, healing, and restoration. Jesus is the fulfillment of all prophecies related to the Messiah. He was:

- The Son of God
- The seed of Eve, Abraham, Isaac, and David
- Born of a virgin
- Born in Bethlehem of Judea
- Anointed with the Holy Spirit
- A prophet like unto Moses
- A miracle worker
- Forsaken and betrayed for thirty pieces of silver
- A suffering servant
- Crucified
- Mocked
- Forsaken by God
- Pierced
- Not subject to broken bones
- Resurrected
- Our heavenly priest

- The chief cornerstone of the church[6]

Also:

- Jesus now sits at the right hand of the Father.
- His government is righteous.
- His dominion is universal.
- His kingdom is everlasting.[7]

The highest number of prophecies was reserved for the most important person ever to be born—for the salvation of all rests in One—Jesus Christ.

Forth-telling

If foretelling is predicting the future, then forth-telling is causing it. Forth-telling is calling things as they truly are or were meant to be.

Prophecy has the power to create life. God has enabled people to emulate His nature when they prophesy. Paul talks about Abraham as the father of many nations: "As it is written: 'I have made you a father of many nations.' He is our father in the sight of God, in whom he believed—the God who gives life to the dead and calls into being things that were not" (Romans 4:17).

When Abram was ninety-nine years old, God encountered

6 Psalm 2:7, Genesis 3:15; 17:7; 21:12; Psalm 132:11, Isaiah 7:14, Micah 5:2, Psalm 45:7, Isaiah 11:2, 61:1, Deuteronomy 18:15-18, Isaiah 33:5-6, Zechariah 11:12; 13:7, Isaiah 53, Psalm 22:16, Psalm 22:7-8, Psalm 22:1, Zechariah 12:10, Exodus 12:46, Psalm 34:20, Psalm 16:10, Isaiah 26:19, Zechariah 6:13, Isaiah 28:16

7 Psalm 110:1 Psalm 45:6-7 Psalm 72:8; Daniel 7:14 Isaiah 9:7; Daniel 7:14

him saying, "No longer will you be called Abram; your name will be Abraham, for I have made you a father of many nations" (Genesis 17:5).

God "prophesied" to Abram, calling him a father of many nations before Abram had a child with his wife. That is why Paul described God as the One who gives life to the dead and calls things that are not as though they were. Prophetic ministry encompasses the same idea. When we speak the words of the Spirit, we can give life and actually declare things into being that did not exist before. The clearest example of this is when the Lord commanded Ezekiel to prophesy to some dry bones. God said to His prophet,

> Prophesy to these bones and say to them, "Dry bones, hear the word of the LORD! This is what the Sovereign LORD says to these bones: I will make breath enter you, and you will come to life. I will attach tendons to you and make flesh come upon you and cover you with skin; I will put breath in you, and you will come to life. Then you will know that I am the LORD."
>
> —Ezekiel 37:4-6

As Ezekiel was speaking or prophesying, the bones literally came together with tendons, flesh, and skin. He prophesied breath into them and they came to life. What had once been dry and lifeless bones had become a mighty army, simply because Ezekiel prophesied over them. God could have done this without Ezekiel, but I believe He used the prophet to demonstrate what is possible through obedience, faith, and partnership with Him.

I was praying once for a couple that was having trouble getting pregnant. As I was praying, I felt the Lord say they would become pregnant and have a child within one year. I took a step of faith, declared over them what I heard the Lord say, and today they are the proud parents of a healthy baby girl.

I heard a respected prophet share a similar testimony. When the Lord said to tell a couple they were going to have a baby, the prophet did not want to do it because he knew how much hardship the couple had faced with their infertility. God immediately said to him, "If you don't declare it, they will not get pregnant!" He obeyed the Lord and prophesied over the couple, and they had a healthy baby one year later.

Prophecy is about partnering with the purposes of the Father. Our words and declarations carry supernatural grace when coupled with the power of the Holy Spirit. As we draw closer to His heart, we will learn how to call things into being. God is longing for His children to prophesy encouragement, life, and destiny so light will shine forth into the dark places of this world.

The office of prophet versus the gift of prophecy

The most common designation of a religious leader in a Christian church today is that of a pastor. This office or position derives from Ephesians:

> [He] gave gifts to his people . . . So Christ himself gave the apostles, the prophets, the evangelists, the pastors and teachers, to equip his people for works of service, so that the body of Christ may be built up until we all reach unity in the faith and in the knowledge of the Son of God and become mature, attaining to the whole measure of the fullness of Christ.
>
> —Ephesians 4:7-13

According to this passage, Jesus gave a special grace to people in the form of gifts when He ascended to heaven. These gifts enable people to function in a leadership role as an apostle, prophet, evangelist, pastor, or teacher.[8] Each office is a divine calling.

Just as with any of the other five-fold ministries listed in Ephesians 4, there is a difference between the God-ordained office and the spiritual gift. All Christians have the ability to prophesy and are encouraged to grow in the prophetic. Paul said, "Follow the way of love and eagerly desire gifts of the Spirit, especially prophecy" (1 Corinthians 14:1). Later in verse 31, he added, "For you can all prophesy in turn so that everyone may be instructed and encouraged."

So on the one hand, we may all operate in the gift of prophecy; on the other hand, only God chooses who will actually have the call/office of a prophet. This divine call should be recognized by the church in order for the prophet

8 There is also an interpretation that says the gifts Christ gave to people were actually other people called to one of the five specific offices. Kris Vallotton, Basic Training for the Prophetic Ministry (Shippensburg, PA: Destiny Image, 2005) 23.

to properly operate in the office. Jeremiah is an example of a prophet chosen by God. The Lord spoke directly to him, saying, "Before I formed you in the womb I knew you, before you were born I set you apart; I appointed you as a prophet to the nations" (Jeremiah 1:5).

It is important to understand the distinction between the gift of prophecy and the office of a prophet. The gift of prophecy is a manifestation of the Holy Spirit given to individual believers to strengthen the body of Christ.[9] The office of a prophet is a calling from the Lord, recognized by the body, to a specific governmental position in the church in order to train and equip believers to do the work of ministry.

Regardless of whether we have the gift of prophecy or are divinely called to the office of prophet, we are all meant to prophesy.

One may operate in the gift of prophecy but not necessarily be a prophet. People called to the office of prophet will, by nature of that office, also operate in the gift of prophecy. Regardless of whether we have the gift of prophecy or are divinely called to the office of prophet, we are all meant to prophesy. This is worth repeating: Everyone is called to prophesy, but only some are called to be prophets. Though the majority of believers are not set apart as prophets, all have the potential to prophesy.

9 1 Corinthians 12:10

If prophecy is a gift of the Spirit, shouldn't only the gifted people prophesy?

Faith is listed as a gift of the Spirit, but we are all called to believe even if we may not have the gift. An individual may not have the gift of prophecy, but that does not disqualify him from prophesying. Those who do not have particular gifts are commanded to seek after them, especially the gift of prophecy.[10] Many people falsely believe that if they are not born with a particular spiritual gift, they will never have it. While some spiritual gifts may be given at birth, we still have opportunities to get more gifts throughout our lives. We receive gifts by asking. Jesus once said:

> "Which of you fathers, if your son asks for a fish, will give him a snake instead? Or if he asks for an egg, will give him a scorpion? If you then, though you are evil, know how to give good gifts to your children, how much more will your Father in heaven give the Holy Spirit to those who ask him!"
>
> —Luke 11:11-13

James said we don't have gifts because we don't ask God for them.[11] If my children ask me for something, I am usually more than willing to give it to them. If they asked me for a gift they planned to use to bless other people, I would not

10 cf. 1 Corinthians 14:1

11 James 4:2

only provide it but would also be very proud of them. Our heavenly Father is the same way. He enjoys pouring out gifts to His children, especially if they are going to use them for the strengthening, encouragement, and comfort of others. Let us seek and ask the Father for more grace and the gift of prophecy!

If you do not feel like you have the gift of prophecy but would like to, just take a moment to ask the Father right now or simply read this prayer aloud:

> Dear Father God,
>
> Thank You for being the best dad in the whole world. You love to lavish gifts upon your children. Daddy, right now I ask for the gift of prophecy. I desire the ability to speak words of life, power, wisdom, and grace into other people. As I hold out my hands, I receive this gift through the Holy Spirit and trust in faith that You will teach me how to prophesy with love and boldness. In Jesus' name, amen!

CHAPTER 2
The Origins of Prophecy

What comes to mind when you hear the word "prophet" or "prophecy"—maybe a desert dweller with wide eyes and wild hair? For many people, the word "prophet" conjures up just such an individual from an ancient time, who speaks a message from God—a message usually full of condemnation and warning. For several of the Old Testament prophets, this stereotype is not far from the truth.

The Old Testament is full of prophets; in fact, an entire

section of the Scriptures is specifically organized by major and minor prophets. These books include Isaiah, Jeremiah, Lamentations, Ezekiel, Daniel, Hosea, Joel, Amos, Obadiah, Jonah, Micah, Nahum, Habakkuk, Zephaniah, Haggai, Zechariah, and Malachi. (The designations of major and minor refer to the length of the book, not necessarily the importance of the prophet.) Reading about these men, some have developed perceptions of what prophets might be like: super-holy, austere, reclusive, judgmental, moody, and downright strange.

Often our knowledge of prophets is relegated to Sunday School stories and an occasional sermon referencing a passage from one of these books. Growing up in the Church, the only understanding of prophets and prophecy I acquired was a mysterious and almost mythical perception of prophetic ministry isolated to a time period before Jesus. Special individuals were chosen to interpret dreams, predict the future, and perform bizarre symbolic acts as instructed by God—like walking around naked for three years, cooking food over human waste, and even marrying a prostitute.[1]

> The truth is, prophetic ministry is still essential and is meant to be carried on until Christ returns.

After Jesus was born, it seemed prophets were unnecessary and God had ceased to use them to communicate with

1 cf. Ezekiel 4:12; Isaiah 20:3; Hosea 1:2

His people. My erroneous thinking was strengthened by a misinterpretation of Jesus' own words that the Prophets and the Law only prophesied until John.[2] Jesus said He did not come to abolish the Law and the Prophets, but that He came to fulfill them.[3] I falsely believed there were no more prophets because they were no longer necessary.

The truth is, prophetic ministry is still essential and is meant to be carried on until Christ returns. God raised up prophets after Jesus ascended to heaven, and He continues to do so in order to proclaim His kingdom and guide the church into the fullness of her destiny. In fact, Paul declared that the five-fold ministry is meant to "to equip his people for works of service, so that the body of Christ may be built up until we all reach unity in the faith and in the knowledge of the Son of God and become mature, attaining to the whole measure of the fullness of Christ" (Ephesians 4:12-13).

Prophets in the Old Testament

Abraham was the first individual to be officially called a prophet in the Bible.[4] (Enoch was said to have prophesied, but it is unclear whether he was designated as a prophet).[5] Perusing the Old Testament, we find several people called prophets whose writings are not in the Scriptures, including: Aaron, Miriam, Deborah, Samuel, Gad, Nathan, Ahijah, Jehu, Elijah, Elisha, Shemaiah, Iddo, and Micaiah. There were countless others, many of whom were not named. Prophets

2 Matthew 11:13; Luke 16:16

3 Matthew 5:17

4 Genesis 20:7

5 Jude 14

were important characters in the unfolding of God's plan throughout ancient history. In fact, Amos says, "Surely the Sovereign LORD does nothing without revealing his plan to his servants the prophets" (Amos 3:7). Prophets were so important that the Creator of the entire universe always spoke to them before taking action.

Why were prophets even necessary?

Prophets are intermediaries or spokespeople who transmit messages between God and humanity. Prophets were not always present in human history. There were no prophets in the Garden of Eden because the Lord spoke freely with Adam and Eve. It wasn't until they sinned and became separated from God that prophets were needed to bridge the communication gap. We see a key example of this in Exodus 19 and 20.

Moses was a true Old Testament prophet who foreshadowed the ministry of Jesus; he fellowshipped with God intimately and ministered to the Israelite people with signs and wonders, leading them out of Egyptian bondage into freedom. The Lord spoke to Moses in the desert at Mount Sinai. Moses recounted,

> On the morning of the third day there was thunder and lightning, with a thick cloud over the mountain, and a very loud trumpet blast. Everyone in the camp trembled. Then Moses led the people out of the camp to meet with God, and they stood at the foot of the mountain. Mount Sinai was covered with

> smoke, because the LORD descended on it in fire. The smoke billowed up from it like smoke from a furnace, and the whole mountain trembled violently. As the sound of the trumpet grew louder and louder, Moses spoke and the voice of God answered him.
>
> —Exodus 19:16-19

> When the people saw the thunder and lightning and heard the trumpet and saw the mountain in smoke, they trembled with fear. They stayed at a distance and said to Moses,
>
> "Speak to us yourself and we will listen. But do not have God speak to us or we will die."
>
> Moses said to the people, "Do not be afraid. God has come to test you, so that the fear of God will be with you to keep you from sinning."
>
> —Exodus 20:18-21

The Israelites were so afraid of God's manifest presence that they did not want to have direct fellowship with Him. They mistakenly thought they would die if God spoke to them, so they told Moses to be their representative. The people remained at a distance while Moses approached the thick darkness which carried the presence of the Lord. Fear destroyed the opportunity for each Israelite to have personal intimacy with the Lord and, in one sense, elevated prophetic ministry over individual communication with God. Moses explained this:

> When you heard the voice out of the darkness, while the mountain was ablaze with fire, all the leaders of your tribes and your elders came to me. And you said, "The LORD our God has shown us his glory and his majesty, and we have heard his voice from the fire. Today we have seen that a person can live even if God speaks with them. But now, why should we die? This great fire will consume us, and we will die if we hear the voice of the LORD our God any longer. For what mortal has ever heard the voice of the living God speaking out of fire, as we have, and survived? Go near and listen to all that the LORD our God says. Then tell us whatever the LORD our God tells you. We will listen and obey."
>
> —Deuteronomy 5:23-27

Fear destroyed the opportunity for each Israelite to have personal intimacy with the Lord and, in one sense, elevated prophetic ministry over individual communication with God.

The Jewish people chose to listen to a man speak the words of God rather than to hear the voice of God directly. Fear led them to embrace religion over relationship. Although the fear of the Lord is foundational to our knowledge of Him, we were never meant to remain at that level. Awe, humility, and honor are stepping stones to growing in love with the Father. A relationship based solely on fear cannot produce true intimacy. The Lord chose to grant the Israelites' request for an intermediary, but it was not His original intent. Moses expressed the heart of God in Numbers 11:29 when he declared, "I wish that all the Lord's people were prophets and that the Lord would put his Spirit on them!"

Jesus opened the door for Moses' wish to come true through His sacrifice on the cross. Those who accept Christ receive the Holy Spirit and have the ability to prophesy!

The true prophet

In Deuteronomy 18:15, 18-22, God laid out the stipulations of the prophetic office:

> The LORD your God will raise up for you a prophet like me from among you, from your fellow Israelites. You must listen to him . . .
>
> I will raise up for them a prophet like you from among their fellow Israelites, and I will put my words in his mouth. He will tell them everything I command him. I myself will call to account anyone who does not listen to my

words that the prophet speaks in my name.

But a prophet who presumes to speak in
my name anything I have not commanded,
or a prophet who speaks in the name of
other gods, is to be put to death.

You may say to yourselves, "How can we know
when a message has not been spoken by the LORD?"
If what a prophet proclaims in the name of the
LORD does not take place or come true, that is a
message the LORD has not spoken. That prophet
has spoken presumptuously, so do not be alarmed.

Here are the principles we can take from this passage:

- God raised up prophets from His people.
- God put His words in the prophets' mouths.
- The prophets told the people everything they were commanded in the name of the Lord.
- The people were accountable to obey the prophets' words.
- Some prophets would not speak the words of the Lord or would even speak in the names of other gods.
- Those prophets who spoke falsely were to be put to death.
- The test of a prophet's authenticity was whether the prophet's word took place/came true.

All the prophets in the Old Testament were subject to these guidelines, and people eventually became accustomed to the ministry of a prophet. The Jews also understood this passage to be a promise concerning the coming Messiah; for example in John 1:19-23, when John the Baptist began to preach, he was asked if he was "the Prophet":

> Now this was John's testimony when the Jewish leaders in Jerusalem sent priests and Levites to ask him who he was. He did not fail to confess, but confessed freely, "I am not the Messiah."
>
> They asked him, "Then who are you? Are you Elijah?"
>
> He said, "I am not."
>
> "Are you the Prophet?"
>
> He answered, "No."
>
> Finally they said, "Who are you? Give us an answer to take back to those who sent us. What do you say about yourself?"
>
> John replied in the words of Isaiah the prophet, "I am the voice of one calling in the wilderness, 'Make straight the way for the Lord,'"

The Jews clearly expected a specific personal fulfillment of Isaiah's prophecy. When John the Baptist started his ministry, people thought he was the Prophet. John vehemently denied their claim and directed them to Jesus.

As Jesus continued to minister with power and authority, the Jews began to recognize Jesus as the Prophet. When people witnessed the feeding of the five thousand, they began to say to one another, "Surely this is the Prophet who is to come into the world" (John 6:14). Later on, after hearing Jesus speak, the crowds exclaimed, "Surely this man is the Prophet" (John 7:40).

Peter taught that Jesus Christ was the fulfillment of Isaiah's prophecy. He proclaimed:

> Repent, then, and turn to God, so that your sins may be wiped out, that times of refreshing may come from the Lord, and that he may send the Messiah, who has been appointed for you—even Jesus. Heaven must receive him until the time comes for God to restore everything, as he promised long ago through his holy prophets. For Moses said, "The Lord your God will raise up for you a prophet like me from among your own people; you must listen to everything he tells you. Anyone who does not listen to him will be completely cut off from their people." Indeed, beginning with Samuel, all the prophets who have spoken have foretold these days.
>
> —Acts 3:19-24

Jesus not only fulfilled the prophecy of Deuteronomy 18,

he ushered in a new season of prophetic ministry. In the Old Testament, the Holy Spirit would come upon a person and he or she would prophesy. The only way to determine the authenticity of the prophecy and the prophet was to wait and see whether the prophetic word came to pass. The Jews had the authority to judge prophets, so if a word didn't happen, the people were allowed to stone the prophet.

Under the new covenant, the Holy Spirit resides in all believers because of Christ's sacrifice on the cross; thus, everyone is able to prophesy. Thankfully, we do not have to throw rocks anymore. Christians now judge the prophetic word or spirit of the prophecy, and not necessarily the prophet. Jesus, the Prophet, marked a turning point in prophetic history when the covenant of the law was fulfilled and the covenant of grace began.

Prophecy under the new covenant

Many times in the Old Testament, prophets declared the anger and wrath of God due to human sin. Some have termed this type of ministry as "doom and gloom" prophecy, but Paul taught us that our prophetic ministry under the new covenant is no longer about delivering condemnation for sin. He wrote:

Jesus, the Prophet, marked a turning point in prophetic history when the covenant of the law was fulfilled and the covenant of grace began.

> All this is from God, who reconciled us to himself through Christ and gave us the ministry of reconciliation: that God was reconciling the world to himself in Christ, not counting people's sins against them. And he has committed to us the message of reconciliation. We are therefore Christ's ambassadors, as though God were making his appeal through us. We implore you on Christ's behalf: Be reconciled to God. God made him who had no sin to be sin for us, so that in him we might become the righteousness of God.
>
> —2 Corinthians 5:18-21

The gospel is good news of great joy! Jesus came to reconcile people to the Father and to undo the works of the enemy. Believers under the new covenant have the privilege to prophesy and to declare forgiveness of sins, reconciliation with the Father, and intimacy with the Holy Spirit through Jesus Christ. Christians are ambassadors with a heavenly message of glory. This is not to say that prophecy cannot contain warnings or rebukes, but the primary message of prophetic ministry should be one of encouragement and comfort for the purpose of drawing people closer to the Father. Paul teaches that "God's kindness is intended to lead you to repentance" (Romans 2:4). Prophecy is meant to renew our minds through demonstrations of the goodness and grace of the Lord.

If prophecy is still for today, why isn't it prevalent?

Cessationism is a belief that the gifts of the Holy Spirit (including prophecy) have ceased and were practiced only in early church history. Cessationists generally believe the miraculous gifts were only given for the foundation of the church so that the gospel message could be authenticated. As the church became more established, and the canonization of the Bible was being finalized (in the fourth century), focus shifted away from the spiritual gifts and onto Scripture—which became the sole means for spreading the gospel. This resulted in a decline of divine healings, miracles, deliverance, and the prophetic ministry. Eventually people developed theories and theologies explaining why those gifts were no longer in existence or only occurred on rare occasions. The understanding of salvation became mistakenly limited to *believing* in Jesus as Lord and Savior.

Salvation defined

Many people understand salvation as the process of repenting from sins and confessing Jesus Christ as Lord and Savior in order to receive eternal life in heaven. Although this is one aspect of salvation, it is incomplete. *Sozo* is a Greek word meaning to save or make whole.[6] It is a term used many times in the gospels, not just in the context of eternal salvation but also for healing and deliverance.[7] Jesus used *sozo*

6 Strong's Lexicon G4982, http://www.blueletterbible.org/lang/lexicon/lexicon.cfm?Strongs=G4982&t=KJV

7 cf. Matthew 1:21; 9:21-22; Luke 8:36; 17:19; John 3:17; 12:47, et al

to describe His own call when He said that the Son of Man came to seek and to save [sozo] that which was lost.[8]

Jesus demonstrated that salvation was more than just an affirmation of His divinity and reconciliation to the Father. God anointed Jesus with the Holy Spirit to undo the works of the enemy through healing, deliverance, and the prophetic so that people could be free and experience wholeness.[9]

Christ's purpose was prophesied many years before He was even born.[10] Jesus quoted this prophecy in the synagogue when He first began His ministry:

> The Spirit of the Lord is on me, because he has anointed me to proclaim good news to the poor. He has sent me to proclaim freedom for the prisoners and recovery of sight for the blind, to set the oppressed free, to proclaim the year of the Lord's favor.
>
> —Luke 4:18-19

A few verses later, Jesus referred to Himself as a prophet who was not accepted in His own hometown.[11] Even though the Jews knew of Isaiah's prophecy concerning the Messiah, many still had difficulty recognizing Jesus as its fulfillment. Jesus' own relative and forerunner, John the Baptist, experienced doubts while in prison. In Luke 7:19, John had two of his disciples ask Jesus, "Are you the one who is to come, or should we expect someone else?" Jesus responded by saying:

8 Luke 19:10

9 Cf. Acts 10:38

10 Isaiah 61:1-2

11 Luke 4:24

> Go and report to John what you have seen and heard: the blind receive sight, the lame walk, the lepers are cleansed, and the deaf hear, the dead are raised up, the poor have the gospel preached to them. Blessed is he who does not take offense at Me.
>
> —Luke 7:21-23, NASB

Jesus' ministry was to preach the gospel, heal and deliver people, and prophesy. He taught His disciples how to preach the gospel, heal and deliver people, and prophesy. We are called to do the same. Jesus demonstrated that salvation was not just about getting into heaven but also about living in a way that brought heaven to earth.

Commission impossible?

The Great Commission is one of the last recorded commands Jesus gave to His eleven remaining disciples before His ascension. He said to them:

> All authority in heaven and on earth has been given to me. Therefore go and make disciples of all nations, baptizing them in the name of the Father and of the Son and of the Holy Spirit, and teaching them to obey everything I have commanded you.
>
> —Matthew 28:18-20

The disciples were called to teach others to obey everything Jesus had commanded them to do. The mandate Christ charged His followers to embrace required/requires supernatural power to fulfill it. Jesus told His disciples to "heal the sick, raise the dead, cleanse those who have leprosy, drive out demons" (Matthew 10:8). Believers cannot obey this directive unless empowered by the Holy Spirit.

In human terms, the Christian life is not difficult; it is impossible. We are incapable of performing the miracles of Jesus by our own power, but whenever God commands us to do something, He always provides the means for us to accomplish it. The Holy Spirit enables us to do things we are incapable of doing on our own. Faith, intimacy, and risk are required to activate the supernatural potential resident within every Christian.

Unfortunately, many believers are not tapping into the supernatural resources available to them through the Holy Spirit. Much of the church is content to exercise a powerless Christianity by relying on human intelligence, ingenuity, and effort. Paul spoke against this lack when he wrote the kingdom of God is about power, not talk.[12] Our call is too great to neglect the gifts of the Holy Spirit!

The gifts of the Spirit still exist. Espousing cessationism or not, we are practicing it if we live without the supernatural gifts of the Holy Spirit. God's gifts and call are irrevocable.[13] Prophecy is still for today! The Father is waiting for His children to embrace their identities as sons and daughters of the

12 1 Corinthians 4:20

13 Romans 11:29

King and to realize that everything their Father has is at their disposal. As we rise up to fulfill our destiny, let us be like Paul when he told the Corinthians that he didn't preach with wise and persuasive words but with a demonstration of the Spirit's power, so that they would not trust in a man's wisdom, but in God's power.[14] May we learn how to demonstrate the Spirit's power through the ministry of prophecy.

14 1 Corinthians 2:4-5

CHAPTER 3

Obstacles to the Prophetic

Anyone who has ever tried to cultivate a healthy prayer life knows there are usually hurdles to overcome in order to maintain consistency and growth. It is important to rid ourselves of distractions, unconfessed sins, and even improper beliefs about the nature of God. In the same way, stepping into the prophetic requires navigating around obstacles that hinder the experience of true prophetic ministry. This chapter will explore some of the common obstructions to the prophetic.

False beliefs and theology

If you believe something does not exist, you will live according to that belief. If you are driving on a road and see a "Bridge Out Ahead" sign, you will, naturally, try to find another way to get to your destination; but what if the bridge was repaired and nobody had changed the sign? Many people would continue to believe the inaccurate sign. They would miss out on something designed to help them arrive at their intended destination. False beliefs or incorrect theology hinder us from living life the way we were meant to live it.

When I discussed cessationism in the previous chapter, I recognized that there are people who believe the supernatural gifts of the Holy Spirit are no longer functioning. A few passages are commonly cited to refute the existence of prophets and prophetic ministry today. These include, but are not limited to, the following:

- "The law and the prophets were until John." (Luke 16:16, NKJV)
- "Consequently, you are no longer foreigners and strangers, but fellow citizens with God's people and also members of his household, built on the foundation of the apostles and prophets, with Christ Jesus himself as the chief cornerstone." (Ephesians 2:19-20)
- "Love never fails. But where there are prophecies, they will cease; where there are tongues, they will be stilled; where there is knowledge, it will pass away. For

we know in part and we prophesy in part, but when completeness comes, what is in part disappears." (1 Corinthians 13:8-10)

- "In the past God spoke to our ancestors through the prophets at many times and in various ways, but in these last days he has spoken to us by his Son, whom he appointed heir of all things, and through whom also he made the universe." (Hebrews 1:1-2)

Going through each passage is beyond the scope of this book, but none of these verses actually teach that prophetic ministry or the office of prophet has ceased. Although people may use scriptures to discount the prophetic for today, there are actually numerous passages in the New Testament that support prophetic ministry. Perhaps the clearest text is from Acts 2, when the Holy Spirit came on Pentecost. The believers were filled with the Holy Spirit and started declaring the wonders of God in different languages. Some of the people who witnessed this were amazed, while others dismissed the believers as being drunk. Peter stood up and addressed the crowd, saying:

> Fellow Jews and all of you who live in Jerusalem, let me explain this to you; listen carefully to what I say. These people are not drunk, as you suppose. It's only nine in the morning! No, this is what was spoken by the prophet Joel:
>
> "In the last days, God says, I will pour out my Spirit

> on all people. Your sons and daughters will prophesy, your young men will see visions, your old men will dream dreams. Even on my servants, both men and women, I will pour out my Spirit in those days, and they will prophesy. I will show wonders in the heavens above and signs on the earth below, blood and fire and billows of smoke. The sun will be turned to darkness and the moon to blood before the coming of the great and glorious day of the Lord. And everyone who calls on the name of the Lord will be saved."
>
> —Acts 2:13-21

Peter was quoting the Old Testament prophet Joel and applying that prophecy to the present moment. With the death and resurrection of Christ, history entered the season of the last days. No longer would the Spirit of the Lord come upon a select few to prophesy; God would instead pour out His Spirit on all flesh—regardless of age, gender, nationality, or social rank. The result of this outpouring would be the ability of all to prophesy. Visions and dreams would also increase.

We continue to live in the last days. The Holy Spirit is available to all those who desire Him. Scripture teaches that prophecy is a gift of the Spirit,[1] all may prophesy,[2] and prophets existed even after Jesus ascended into heaven.[3] Jesus said that he would send us prophets, along with wise men and teachers.[4]

1 1 Corinthians 12:10

2 1 Corinthians 14:31

3 Acts 13:1

4 Matthew 23:34

Fear

Another obstacle to prophetic ministry is fear. When we succumb to anxiety or worry, we are held back from walking in the fullness of our destiny. Unfortunately, fear often comes in many forms and subtle ways. Here are a few of the more common types:

☙ *Fear of looking foolish*

Fear of what other people think often disguises itself as wisdom. Prudence, caution, carefulness, discretion, rationality, and thoughtfulness—although important in the right circumstances—may actually be shields people use to protect their public images. Many people do not step out into the prophetic because they are afraid of looking foolish, extreme, or crazy. Prophetic ministry does not have to be strange or garish, but there will always be some who look at it with a critical and suspecting eye.

Just as David danced before the ark wearing only a linen ephod, ignoring the ire of his wife,[5] our main concern should be the Lord and not how other people may view us. This is not to say we should prophesy without our clothes on, but rather we should have the same heart as David. He replied to his wife Michal, "I will become even more undignified than this, and I will be humiliated in my own eyes" (2 Samuel 6:22).

Paul was not ashamed of the gospel, and he did not let

5 2 Samuel 6

Greek or Jewish opinion sway him from ministering.[6] We must learn to discern genuine wisdom from the selfish fear of public opinion.

A contemporary prophet was eating at a restaurant. He heard God tell him to go over to a man sitting at another table and nibble on his ear. At first the prophet argued with the Lord because it seemed like such a foolish thing to do, but he had cultivated such an intimate relationship with the Father that he finally obeyed. The prophet went over and sat down next to this stranger and started nibbling on his ear!

The man broke down in tears and explained that his wife had recently died. She was a Christian and he still wasn't. He used to let her talk to him about the Gospel . . . but only if she would nibble on his ear. After she passed away, he said the only way he would ever listen to anyone preach the gospel was if someone nibbled on his ear first! This prophet was able to push past his fear to enable this widowed man to experience a divine encounter with the Father's love.

☙ *Fear of being deceived*

Another fear preventing believers from pursuing prophetic ministry is the fear of being deceived or doing something wrong. Many times in Scripture we are told to be on guard against false prophets. Unfortunately, people have sometimes taken these warnings to the extreme and have rejected any form of prophecy for fear of being tricked or of participating in a sinful activity. However, the fact that we are warned against false prophets implies there are also true,

6 Romans 1:16

godly prophets. There would not be a great need to caution believers against false prophets if there were no true prophets. False prophets do exist, but we should not let them hinder us from engaging in the prophetic.

The world has a myriad of counterfeits to genuine prophetic ministry. Some of these include fortune-telling, palm reading, astrology, divination, witchcraft, and even Ouija boards. The reason there are so many counterfeits of the prophetic is because the enemy recognizes the great value of true prophecy. A smart criminal does not waste time making fake pennies; he only counterfeits large banknotes. Our job as the church is to discern what is from the Lord—to rely on the Holy Spirit to guide us into all truth.

The reason there are so many counterfeits of the prophetic is because the enemy recognizes the great value of true prophecy.

Fear of the unknown

My young son is fairly set in his ways when it comes to eating. He loves certain foods and is wary of anything that looks or smells strange—especially if it is green. His mother and I try to encourage him to sample new dishes because he is missing some amazing and nutritious cuisine. My son is not unique in this behavior. People have a tendency to fear what they do not know. False beliefs, misconceptions, and myths usually arise when there is a lack of good information.

Apostles, prophets, pastors, teachers, and evangelists are needed to properly instruct believers about the prophetic. Resources are available. Prophetic ministries throughout the world are growing and equipping believers to step out in prophecy. We have to seek out these resources. It is up to us to get past our fear of the unknown and to experience what God desires us to embrace through prophecy.

☙ *Fear of being wrong*

People who begin in the prophetic commonly fear giving a bad or inaccurate prophetic word. As with any other endeavor, we cannot let the fear of failure deter us from practicing prophecy. Mistakes can actually be valuable tools to sharpen, guide, and spur us to greater mastery. Prophecy is a gift from our Father. He does not expect us to use it perfectly at first.

Risk is required to exercise our faith and enter into the fullness of our prophetic destinies.

Risk is required to exercise our faith and enter into the fullness of our prophetic destinies. Fear is certainly one of the major hindering blocks to growing in the prophetic but God did not give us a spirit of fear, but he did give us the Spirit "...of power, and of love, and of a sound mind" (2 Tim. 1:7). May we choose not to concede to fear but rather to partner with the Holy Spirit and boldly declare the wonders of God to the world!

The religious spirit

Jerusalem was not known for accepting prophets; it was known for destroying them. It is interesting that Jesus reserved His harshest rebukes for the religious leaders of Israel. Jesus said to them:

> "You snakes! You brood of vipers! How will you escape being condemned to hell? Therefore I am sending you prophets and wise men and teachers. Some of them you will kill and crucify; others you will flog in your synagogues and pursue from town to town. And so upon you will come all the righteous blood that has been shed on earth, from the blood of righteous Abel to the blood of Zechariah son of Berekiah, whom you murdered between the temple and the altar. I tell you the truth, all this will come upon this generation. O Jerusalem, Jerusalem, you who kill the prophets and stone those sent to you, how often I have longed to gather your children together, as a hen gathers her chicks under her wings, but you were not willing."
>
> —Matthew 23:33-37

The well-trained, educated, and established men who were charged with leading the Jewish people closer to the Lord actually rejected and crucified Him in the flesh.

The spirit of religion hinders people from engaging in prophetic ministry. This spirit is antagonistic and violent towards the Holy Spirit. It causes our focus to shift from reconciliation to rules, from the heart to external appearance. God is not interested in religion; He desires relationship. Jesus told us to love him with all our heart, with all our understanding, and with all our strength, and that loving our neighbors is more important than all the burnt offerings and sacrifices we can bring Him.[7] A humble and contrite heart is required to position ourselves to properly receive prophets and prophecy. The church must learn to identify the religious spirit and cast it out, wherever it may be present.

> We have the responsibility and mandate from God to embrace truth, shun fear, and promote a spirit of love and humility over religion.

Perhaps you can take a moment right now and ask the Holy Spirit if you have a religious spirit. If you sense that you do, simply ask God to forgive you and renounce it. You can pray this simple prayer:

Father God,

I ask Your forgiveness for harboring a religious spirit. I renounce this legalistic and judgmental attitude and ask You to give me a heart to receive and embrace prophecy. Holy Spirit, renew my mind to understand Your ways and prevent anything from hindering me in the prophetic. In Jesus' name, amen!

7 Mark 12:33

Overcoming obstacles through repentance

Understanding the obstacles to prophetic ministry equips us to confront and remove them. We have the responsibility and mandate from God to embrace truth, shun fear, and promote a spirit of love and humility over religion. One of the ways to do this is through repentance.

The Greek word for repentance in the New Testament is *metanoia*, which means to change the way you think.[8] For instance, if a Christian believes he is not spiritual or holy enough to be considered a saint—if he thinks he is a perpetual sinner—then he must repent of his thinking. The Bible teaches us that we are not only saints but also sons and daughters of the King! Anything that hinders the prophetic in our lives is reason to repent and seek guidance from the Holy Spirit. Paul said, "Don't copy the behavior and customs of this world, but let God transform you into a new person by *changing the way you think*. Then you will learn to know God's will for you, which is good and pleasing and perfect" (Romans 12:2, NLT; emphasis added).

As we allow the Lord to renew our minds, we will begin to understand the desires of His heart. False beliefs, fear, and even the religious spirit will not hinder us from speaking words of life. God's will is for His people to prophesy. May no obstacle stand in our way!

8 Strong's Lexicon G3340, http://www.blueletterbible.org/lang/lexicon/lexicon.cfm?Strongs=G3340&t=KJV

CHAPTER 4
Hearing from God

Since prophecy is basically expressing the words we receive from God, it is crucial that we learn how God communicates with us. Our starting point is the understanding that God talks to us. Throughout the Bible, we see the Lord interacting with ordinary men, women, and children. He is a relational God. He demonstrated His desire for connection by sending us His Son, Jesus Christ, as a human.

Christ is Emmanuel—God *with us*, not *far from us*. People are able to interact with the Lord of Lords as if speaking to a friend. The Good Shepherd reassures us that His sheep will hear His voice.[1] Open communication with God should be the foundation of our relationship, not just obedience and adherence to religious principles. James Goll, in his book *The Beginner's Guide to Hearing God,* writes:

> God does not want us to know only the historical Jesus, who came in human form and walked among men. He greatly yearns that we would also know the living, resurrected Christ through the power of the Holy Spirit. The Father wants to enable us to hear, know, and obey the risen Lord. But often we don't realize He is speaking to us. No wonder we miss His cues. He is such a multifaceted Creator, endlessly creative in how He chooses to communicate.[2]

Learning to listen

As a child, I was constantly exposed to classical music because my family loved it. I did not. Whether at home or in the car, I would beg my parents to change the radio station because I thought classical music was boring. When we went to symphony concerts, I would usually fall asleep; the music all sounded the same to me.

Thankfully, my parents persisted in exposing me to classical music. Eventually, I started playing the violin and joining orchestras. I began to enjoy the subtleties of the music. Whereas I once heard a jumbled mess, I began to learn

1 Cf. John 10:1-18

2 James Goll, The Beginner's Guide to Hearing God (Ventura, CA: Regal Books, 2004), 33

to identify specific instruments, follow the rhythm, embrace dynamic nuances, and experience the heart of musical pieces. Today, classical music is my favorite genre. I am moved, inspired, and uplifted by its beauty. It speaks to me.

In a similar way, God's voice is like high art. Though His voice can be unintelligible and strange to untrained senses, those who are willing to pursue Him will soon become more adept at listening to His voice and understanding it. Too often, people get frustrated and stop trying to listen for God's voice after many seemingly failed attempts.

We must embrace truth in order to experience the Truth.

I encourage you to not give up! It is easy to get disheartened and start believing God does not communicate—or you are incapable of hearing Him. Faith then gets reduced to one-sided prayers and religious obedience rather than a relationship based on love and communication. Christianity is about intimacy. Experiencing the Father's presence and hearing His voice must be central.

Lies, myths, and questions

When it comes to listening, our beliefs are crucial. We must embrace truth in order to experience *the* Truth. The veil has been torn. We are a royal priesthood. We are sheep of the Good Shepherd, and we hear His voice.[3]

The primary objective of the enemy is to steal, kill, and

3 Cf. John 14:6; Matthew 27:51; 1 Peter 2:9; John 10

destroy.[4] The Father of Lies looks for every opportunity to deceive us and keep us separated from God. Throughout my life, I have believed or heard others say the following:

- I don't hear from God.
- Only super-spiritual people hear God.
- The Bible is all we need as Christians.
- God doesn't want to talk to me.
- God has more important things to do than to talk with me.
- Only crazy people think they hear from God.
- That's my own voice I'm hearing, not God's.
- God wouldn't say that or ask me to do this.
- Satan is trying to deceive me.

Some of these statements actually possess elements of truth. The enemy attempts to seduce and distort our beliefs so that a real relationship with God seems out of reach. The truth is Jesus Christ. He is perfect theology. He not only demonstrated that an intimate relationship with God was possible—He taught us that it should be our norm.

4 Cf. John 10:10

Daddy loves intimacy

God is not only our heavenly Father but also our "Abba" (the Aramaic word for father).[5] The relationship a child has with his or her daddy is a shadow of what is available to us with God. It is unthinkable for me not to communicate with my own children. I would be neglectful and unloving if I did not speak with them. God is the best daddy ever, and He loves to interact with His children.

What does your relationship with the Father look like? Perhaps the answer to that is best found by asking these questions:

- Are you free to be yourself?
- Do you experience joy in His presence?
- Are you secure in knowing all of your needs are met by Him?
- Are you confident Papa has your best interests in mind?
- Is He always available to you—willing to talk, laugh, and play?

> God is the best Daddy anyone could ever have.

If you believe you have a good Dad, then the answer to all these questions is a resounding yes!

5 cf. Mark 14:36; Romans 8:15; Galatians 4:6

God is the best Daddy anyone could ever have. Even if you have not experienced God this way, it is still possible. We must believe in the goodness of God as a loving Father. Faith is the foundation for our relationship with God.[6] When we approach Him believing He is good, we have opened the door for the Father to prove our faith true. If you have doubts about His nature, ask Abba to reveal Himself to you or pray this simple prayer:

Dear Abba Father,

I declare You are the best daddy in the whole world. Help me to experience You that way. I come to You as Your child, wanting to know Your heart. Encounter me and speak in a way I can hear and understand. Make Your voice known.

Papa, what do You think of me?

Take a moment to listen. What is He saying to you?

Repent of lies and declare the truth

When we believe a lie, we empower the Liar. Lies separate us from God, because God is truth. It is our responsibility to identify any false beliefs we may have and to repent from them. By doing so, we literally change the way we think about lies, and we begin to experience freedom as we declare truth. As Paul taught, "We demolish arguments and every pretension that sets itself up against the knowledge of God, and we

6 Cf. Hebrews 11:6

take captive every thought to make it obedient to Christ" (2 Corinthians 10:5).

Take a moment, right now, and think about any lies you may believe about yourself or God. Ask the Holy Spirit to highlight a particular lie and then repent. For example, if you believe that you do not hear from God, simply declare:

> I repent of the lie that I don't hear from God, and I declare the truth that the Lord is my shepherd and I know His voice.[7]

Continue to do this for all known lies you have believed, or for anything else the Holy Spirit brings to mind.

Positioning ourselves to hear

The book of Luke contrasts how two sisters interacted with Jesus:

> As Jesus and his disciples were on their way, he came to a village where a woman named Martha opened her home to him. She had a sister called Mary, who sat at the Lord's feet listening to what he said. But Martha was distracted . . .
>
> —Luke 10:38-40

7 cf. John 10:1-18

The phrase "sitting at one's feet" meant being a disciple or learner of another individual (Paul sat at Gamaliel's feet).[8]This was a posture of humility that demonstrated a commitment to stay focused, attentive, and open. From this position, Mary listened to Jesus.

Martha remained active, honorably serving the Lord, but she was distracted from hearing what Jesus had to say. Jesus taught that Mary's position was better. Sitting down is a physical act that requires a willful choice to stay still and grounded. This choice to remain in His presence even takes priority over serving Him. We can do great things for God but never develop any real intimacy with Him.[9] As we develop a relationship based on communication, we will do things for Him as lovers and not servants.

"Be still, and know that I am God."

—Psalm 46:10

Silence your environment

Sitting before the Lord can be difficult if we are surrounded by commotion. We will hear God's voice more clearly when we rid our environments of excess noise. We live in a world inundated with an unprecedented level of media in the forms of television, music, movies, Internet, and cell phones. Unplugging ourselves from the clamor of technology and sound can position our spirits to be more attuned to the Holy

8 Acts 22:3

9 cf. Matthew 7:22-23

Spirit.

People know when you are distracted or not fully paying attention to them. Have you ever gotten frustrated trying to have a conversation with someone who is texting or watching TV? Practice giving your undivided heart to God when you spend time with Him. Find a quiet place and get accustomed to the silence. Often, His voice comes through a gentle whisper that can easily be missed if you are not paying attention.

> "Teach me your way, O LORD, and
> I will walk in your truth;
>
> give me an undivided heart, that
> I may fear your name."
>
> —Psalm 86:11

Silence your mind

Even if people turn off the noise in their environments, it is common for them to experience a cacophony of thoughts echoing through their minds. This simple prayer has helped me immensely with that problem:

> God, I ask you to silence every voice in my mind that is not from You, especially my own.

This prayer is a good starting point because I can then proceed to listen, believing in faith that what I hear will be from the Lord.

Experiencing peace of mind may take some practice because our lives can be filled with so much excess. That is why Paul wrote to the Philippians, "Whatever is true, whatever is noble, whatever is right, whatever is pure, whatever is lovely, whatever is admirable—if anything is excellent or praiseworthy—think about such things" (Philippians 4:8). The more our thoughts are centered on God, the better prepared we will be to connect with Him.

> "And the peace of God, which transcends all understanding, will guard your hearts and your minds in Christ Jesus."
>
> —Philippians 4:7

Begin by worshipping God

Once you develop the discipline of sitting still and silent before the Lord, you are free to begin worshipping Him. Worship is not limited to sanctuaries or praise music; it is the intentional turning of your heart and affections toward the Lord. Communicate your love, adoration, and praise

Worship is not limited to sanctuaries or praise music; it is the intentional turning of your heart and affections toward the Lord.

to Him in your own special way. You can express your feelings through almost limitless activities such as singing, dancing, art, journaling, poetry, soaking, playing an instrument, or just talking. It is impossible for your Daddy to not respond.

My three-year-old daughter has a habit of telling secrets to me. She will say, "I have a secret for you." Then she moves close to my ear and whispers, "Love you, Daddy."

It gets me every time. I thank her and then do the same thing to her. Then she wants to do it again, and this goes back and forth for a couple of minutes until we are laughing, snuggling, and kissing. This is the heart of worship. When we come to our Father as a little child, He is naturally drawn to us and eager to whisper secrets in our ears.

> "Therefore, whoever humbles himself like this child is the greatest in the kingdom of heaven"
>
> —Matthew 18:4

Get to know His voice

Perhaps you are reading this while in a quiet place. Take a moment to listen to what's going on around you. Can you hear any singing? Do you realize there is music constantly playing around you? Simply turn on a radio and you will discover songs were always in the airwaves but you needed a special receiver to tune into them. In the same way, God is always speaking, but you need to develop your ability to zero in on His voice.

In the days before caller ID, if someone you didn't know called you, he would have to identify himself. This is not the case with people we know well; we automatically recognize the voices of our close friends and family. God's voice may be strange and foreign at first, but the more we interact with Him, the easier it will be to identify it.

Samuel learned to listen

The story of young Samuel illustrates the need to become familiar with hearing the Lord's voice. Samuel's mother, Hannah, was barren, and she promised to commit a future son to God's service if she could get pregnant. God intervened and Samuel was born. When Samuel was weaned, Hannah fulfilled her pledge and placed Samuel in Eli's care at the temple.

> The boy Samuel ministered before the LORD under Eli. In those days the word of the LORD was rare; there were not many visions. One night Eli, whose eyes were becoming so weak that he could barely see, was lying down in his usual place. The lamp of God had not yet gone out, and Samuel was lying down in the temple of the LORD, where the ark of God was.
>
> Then the LORD called Samuel. Samuel answered, "Here I am." And he ran to Eli and said, "Here I am; you called me."
>
> But Eli said, "I did not call; go back and lie down." So he went and lay down.

> Again the LORD called, "Samuel!" And Samuel got up and went to Eli and said, "Here I am; you called me." "My son," Eli said, "I did not call; go back and lie down." Now Samuel did not yet know the LORD: The word of the LORD had not yet been revealed to him. The LORD called Samuel a third time, and Samuel got up and went to Eli and said, "Here I am; you called me." Then Eli realized that the LORD was calling the boy. So Eli told Samuel, "Go and lie down, and if he calls you, say, 'Speak, LORD, for your servant is listening.'"
>
> So Samuel went and lay down in his place. The LORD came and stood there, calling as at the other times, "Samuel! Samuel!" Then Samuel said, "Speak, for your servant is listening."
>
> —I Samuel 3:1-10

Samuel's story is similar to the experience of many people. Although most believers do not hear the audible voice of God, they do hear from God in many other ways but may attribute His communication to something else. There are times when the Lord speaks, but we do not recognize Him. It is helpful to realize God's first language is probably not English, Spanish, nor any other tongue currently spoken on earth. God does speak in ways we can understand, but it is our responsibility to learn how and what He is speaking at any given moment. We need to learn how to become spiritually multilingual. As Job said:

> For God speaks again and again, though people do not recognize it. He speaks in dreams, in visions of the night, when deep sleep falls on people as they lie in their beds. He whispers in their ears and terrifies them with warnings. He makes them turn from doing wrong; he keeps them from pride. He protects them from the grave, from crossing over the river of death.
>
> —Job 33:14-18

The voice of God

The Lord speaks in different ways. In I Kings 19:11-13, the prophet Elijah had an encounter with God while in a cave at Horeb:

> The LORD said, "Go out and stand on the mountain in the presence of the LORD, for the LORD is about to pass by." Then a great and powerful wind tore the mountains apart and shattered the rocks before the LORD, but the LORD was not in the wind.
>
> After the wind there was an earthquake, but the LORD was not in the earthquake. After the earthquake came a fire, but the LORD was not in the fire.
>
> And after the fire came a gentle whisper.

> When Elijah heard it, he pulled his cloak over his face and went out and stood at the mouth of the cave.
>
> Then a voice said to him, "What are you doing here, Elijah?"

Elijah heard the still small voice of God, albeit right after a destructive hurricane, earthquake, and fire passed by him.

The voice of the Lord boomed from heaven while Jesus was praying:

> Now my heart is troubled, and what shall I say? "Father, save me from this hour?" No, it was for this very reason I came to this hour. Father, glorify your name! Then a voice came from heaven, "I have glorified it, and will glorify it again." The crowd that was there and heard it said it had thundered.
>
> —John 12:27-29

God can speak in a gentle whisper, a thunderous boom, and everything in between. It is interesting, the crowd around Jesus that heard God's voice thought it was only a natural act of weather. The issue was not a matter of volume but of spiritual sensitivity. That is why Jesus continually said, "He who has ears to hear, let him hear."[10]

We should not be asking God to speak up; we should humble our hearts and minds to become more focused on

10 Cf. Matthew 11:15; 13:9; Mark 4:9

listening to what He is saying.

Hearing requires hunger

After Jesus taught the Parable of the Sower, the disciples asked Jesus why he used parables to teach the people. Jesus responded:

> This is why I speak to them in parables: Though seeing, they do not see; though hearing, they do not hear or understand. In them is fulfilled the prophecy of Isaiah: "You will be ever hearing but never understanding; you will be ever seeing but never perceiving." For this people's heart has become calloused; they hardly hear with their ears, and they have closed their eyes. Otherwise they might see with their eyes, hear with their ears, understand with their hearts, and turn, and I would heal them.
>
> —Matthew 13:13-15

Jesus explained that He hid His messages in parables because the people were stubborn and had hardened hearts. At first glance, that would seem like a good reason to be clear and straightforward with them rather than cryptic, but the implication is that even if He had spoken to the people plainly, they would still not have received His message. Jesus taught in parables to *conceal* truth rather than express it more clearly. This is actually a loving action, because if the people understood His message they would be accountable to live it out—something they were not prepared to do. We will be judged according to what we do with that which we have been given.

There were probably also some people in the crowd who genuinely wanted to know and follow Christ. This parable was an appeal for the spiritually hungry to search out answers to the mystery. Whenever we do not understand something about our faith, the Lord always reaches out His hand with a divine invitation for greater intimacy. Those who are earnest will draw close to Jesus and listen for His voice. We are to maintain humble and passionate hearts to know God more, especially when our understanding is limited. Proverbs 25:2 says, "It is the glory of God to conceal a matter; to search out a matter is the glory of kings". Our heavenly Father doesn't hide things *from* us, he hides things *for* us!

Be obedient to what you hear from God

Christians have a responsibility to respond to the Lord's prompting. If we refuse to do what He tells us in one area, we will probably experience difficulty hearing from Him in other areas. In one sense, God is being merciful by not overtly communicating with disobedient believers. If people were to constantly hear from the Lord but never respond, they would be in jeopardy of greater judgment—more is required from those who have been given much.[11] Conversely, when we are faithful to the words we hear from God, He will delight in opening His heart to us even further. God will speak more

11 Luke 12:48

often to those who treasure and respond to His words. May we steward what we hear from the Lord and cultivate hearts of good soil so that His divine revelations will produce fruit.

Never give up

Several other basic principles can help us in hearing our Father's voice. We can fast, repent from known sin, and even go on a retreat. Perhaps the most effective discipline is to spend time with people who consistently hear from God. If you go to a foreign country where you do not speak the language, it would be helpful to find someone who spoke both your language and the foreign language. Such people not only become our translators but also our guides and teachers, equipping us to eventually become fluent in the foreign language. Find believers who have cultivated an intimate relationship with the Spirit—and who are familiar with hearing the Spirit's voice—and, learn from them. Ask them to pray with you and for you.

Finally, don't give up! Be relentless and specific in your prayers and attempts to connect with God. The parable of the persistent widow[12] demonstrates that persistence will be rewarded. Jesus also encourages people to keep asking.[13] We have a Father in heaven who loves to speak to us even more than we long to speak with Him. If we draw near to Him, He will draw near to us.[14] He will run to us, because He loves us as precious sons and daughters.

12 Luke 18:1-8

13 Luke 11:9-13; James 4:2

14 cf. James 4:8

Ask and it will be given to you; seek and you will find; knock and the door will be opened to you. For everyone who asks receives; he who seeks finds; and to him who knocks, the door will be opened.

—Matthew 7:7-8

CHAPTER 5
The Various Ways God Communicates

The Christian walk is not about following a set of principles or about trying to meet certain religious standards; it is about cultivating a love relationship with the Trinity. If a man is in love with a woman who does not speak his language, he will work hard to learn hers. Our love for God should compel us to study the way He communicates. It is actually a fun endeavor. Every nuance, symbol, or revelation we can grasp is another opportunity to connect with our Savior. He is the Creator; creativity is His nature.

Like a dad playing Hide and Go Seek with his child,

God delights in seeing His children seek out the secrets of His heart. He is looking for people who will draw near to Him and get to know Him better. All of us have been given a divine invitation to move into greater intimacy. How we respond is up to us.

The God who reveals Himself

The Father loves to interact with His children and to display His nature to them. All forms of divine communication are revelations. God is choosing to reveal Himself to those He has created. Steve Thompson writes:

> Some types of revelation are of a higher order than others. Lower levels of revelation include mental or spiritual impressions or perceptions, gentle internal visions, and the still, small voice of God that we hear in our spirits. Each of these is a valid type of revelation, albeit lower level. Higher level revelations include open visions, angelic visitations, visitations of the Lord, vivid dreams, trances, being caught up in the Spirit, and other prophetic experiences. As a general rule, the less subjective way in which a revelation comes, the higher level it is.[1]

This chapter will give a brief overview of how God speaks to people through different forms of revelation. This is not an exhaustive list because the Lord can communicate to us through any means He desires.

1 Thompson 37

Scripture

The Bible is one of the most common and universal methods God uses to communicate to people. Hebrews 4:12-13 teaches:

> For the word of God is living and active. Sharper than any double-edged sword, it penetrates even to dividing soul and spirit, joints and marrow; it judges the thoughts and attitudes of the heart. Nothing in all creation is hidden from God's sight. Everything is uncovered and laid bare before the eyes of him to whom we must give account.

The writer of Hebrews teaches us that the word of God is prophetic in nature. The Word can see into our hearts and minds and reveal hidden things. The Holy Spirit not only speaks to us through Scripture, but He also allows us to speak to others on His behalf using Scripture.

God used Scripture to speak to me during one of the lowest points of my life. I was a young Christian when I was faced with the decision of whether to pursue the Lord's call—even though it would mean rejection from my family. I was not familiar with the voice of the Lord yet, but something inside my head said to read Psalm 91.

I rationalized that inner voice by believing it was my mind talking to me—that I somehow already knew this psalm would apply to my particular situation. Immediately, the voice said, "Dave, you don't know any Psalms."

Realizing how true that was, I opened my Bible and saw the study notes summarized Psalm 91 as a "glowing testimony to the security of those who trust in God."[2] It ends with the words:

> "Because he loves me," says the LORD, "I will rescue him; I will protect him, for he acknowledges my name. He will call on me, and I will answer him; I will be with him in trouble, I will deliver him and honor him. With long life I will satisfy him and show him my salvation."
>
> —Psalm 91:14-16

This passage was pivotal to me—it strengthened and encouraged me in that crisis moment of my life. God spoke to me clearly through this psalm and confirmed my call to ministry, even in the midst of opposition. The Lord is faithful to protect, deliver, and provide for all who love Him.

Study, meditate on, and memorize Scripture.[3] The more familiar we become with Scripture, the closer we will travel into the heart of the Father. Our aim is not necessarily to be Bible scholars, but to develop an intimate friendship with the Holy Spirit, who will help us understand the words of Scripture and make them a part of us. "The Word became flesh" (John 1:14) so that flesh could become the Word.

I have heard many stories of people opening the Bible to a random page and God speaking to a specific situation

2 NIV Study Bible (Grand Rapid, MI: Zondervan, 1985) 883.

3 Cf. Psalm 119:9-11

through a particular passage/verse. Although this does occur, it is probably best not to make such a method our general practice when trying to listen for God's voice. We should get in the habit of reading Scripture on a daily basis. It is helpful to listen to Scripture recited, taught, and preached. Paul says that "faith comes through hearing" (Romans 10:17) the word of God. God speaks and we are sustained; we do not live on bread alone, but on every word that comes from the mouth of God.[4]

Impressions

An impression can be defined as a telling image imprinted on the senses or the mind.[5] An impression is a common form of prophetic revelation that comes through the mind, body, or emotions. It can be a thought, picture, physical sensation, or feeling.

Many times, people may experience tingling or pain in their bodies and wonder what is wrong with them, not realizing that God is trying to highlight another person's need that requires attention. For example, one woman entered a store and began to feel depressed for no specific reason. She eventually found out the manager of the store was struggling with grief over a recent loss, so she prayed for him. It is our responsibility to

> The more familiar we become with Scripture, the closer we will travel into the heart of the Father.

4 Deuteronomy 8:3; Matthew 4:4

5 http://www.merriam-webster.com/dictionary/impression

discern such a prophetic impression and to discover whom God may want us to address and how.

Impressions are related to intuition and are sometimes referred to as a sixth sense. In a way this is true, because our five physical senses are connected to our spiritual senses. Just as we can taste, touch, see, hear, and feel with our physical bodies, so can our spirits in the spiritual realm. Elisha's servant learned this firsthand when the Arameans were preparing to attack:

When the servant of the man of God got up and went out early the next morning, an army with horses and chariots had surrounded the city.

> "Oh no, my lord! What shall we
> do?" the servant asked.
>
> "Don't be afraid," the prophet answered.
>
> "Those who are with us are more than those
> who are with them." And Elisha prayed,
> 'Open his eyes, LORD, so that he may see.'
>
> Then the LORD opened the servant's eyes,
> and he looked and saw the hills full of horses
> and chariots of fire all around Elisha.
>
> —2 Kings 6:15-17

The Lord opened the servant's spiritual eyes to see the true reality of his surroundings. This can happen for all spiritual senses. Jesus repeatedly said, "Whoever has ears, let him hear."[6]

This was not a call to clean the wax out of one's ears, but rather a command to activate the spiritual hearing necessary to understand spiritual truth. The Lord is Spirit and His followers worship Him in Spirit and in truth.[7] Ask God to activate your spiritual senses, right now, so you can become more sensitive to the spirit realm.

Inner voice

The still small voice of the Lord is audible—not in our ears but in our minds, hearts, or spirits. That voice may speak just one word, but that one word may have profound impact or meaning. The inner voice does not always have to come in a whisper. Sometimes the Lord speaks very loudly, yet still internally.

One night I asked the Holy Spirit what I should pray for. I immediately heard in my mind, *"Pray for the revivals going on in Japan, India, and the Netherlands"*. I knew a little about the Spirit's move in Japan and India, but I had never heard of anything going on in the Netherlands. I was a little embarrassed to pray for this in front of my wife because it seemed so random.

The next day, I researched online and found an article with the heading "Revival in the Netherlands." A spiritual awakening was taking place in that country, especially among the younger generation. I came to realize it is best not to doubt

6 Cf. Matthew 11:15; 13:9; Mark 4:9
7 Cf. 2 Corinthians 3:17; John 4:23

the Holy Spirit when He speaks to you, even if it is in a quiet voice.

Audible voice

Though it is uncommon, individuals are able to hear God's voice with their physical ears. There are several notable instances of God speaking audibly to people in the Bible:

- Moses heard the Lord's voice from a burning bush.[8]
- The young Samuel did not recognize the audible voice of God calling him in the night until Eli told him it was the Lord.[9]
- A voice from heaven was heard at Jesus' baptism saying, "This is my Son, whom I love; with him I am well pleased" (Matthew 3:17).
- Peter, James, and John heard the same voice when Jesus was transfigured on a mountain.[10]
- Saul heard the resurrected Jesus speak from a flash of light (on his way to Damascus).[11]

God continues to speak audibly to people. Numerous

8 Exodus 3
9 1 Samuel 1:3
10 Luke 9:35
11 Acts 9:4-5

testimonies throughout history attest to the Lord dramatically communicating with men, women, and children. Unfortunately, many people believe God no longer speaks audibly because such instances are fairly uncommon. People even attribute hearing God's voice to mental illness. Often our beliefs will dictate our experiences, or at least our perceptions of them. Regardless of whether we have heard God's audible voice, there is a day approaching when all people will hear it clearly and bow down in reverence.

Dreams

God likes to communicate with people through dreams. Joseph was a dreamer. Daniel interpreted the dreams of King Nebuchadnezzar. Joseph the carpenter only became the earthly father of Jesus because he obeyed a dream. When the Holy Spirit came at Pentecost, Peter stood up to address the crowd and referenced Joel 2:28. He said:

> This is what was spoken by the prophet Joel: "In the last days, God says, I will pour out my Spirit on all people. Your sons and daughters will prophesy, your young men will see visions, your old men will dream dreams."
>
> —Acts 2:16-17

It is important to be open to this type of revelation from God because many people dismiss dreams as strange outputs of one's imagination. Redeem your sleeping hours by making yourself available to hear from the Lord through your dreams. You can steward what you receive from your dreams by writing them down, asking for interpretation, and praying for discernment.

> Our sleeping hours can actually be the most sacred part of the day.

I used to have nightmares as a child. Eventually my mind learned to forget my dreams as soon as I woke up, probably as a way to cope with the unpleasant experiences. By the time I reached college, I had no dream life whatsoever (or if I did, I was not aware of it). It wasn't until later, in adulthood, that God supernaturally restored dreams to me. Instead of having nightmares, I heard the Lord speak to me in dreams.

One vivid dream proved pivotal during a season when I felt God calling my family to move to Redding, CA to attend Bethel's School of Supernatural Ministry. I had completed my ordination requirements for the Presbyterian denomination, was serving in full-time ministry, and had two young children. The thought of moving from southern California to a small northern town, going back to school, and having no job seemed irrational. In my dream, I saw a young woman praying for me. As she was praying she saw luggage, but did not interpret its significance. Then a man standing on a stage with a microphone said he also saw luggage. He immediately declared, "That means you are moving!"

After the dream, I decided to research the school online, because I didn't know much about Bethel Church or its ministry school. On the school's website, I saw a picture of a man and immediately recognized him. He was the man from my dream who had interpreted the meaning of the luggage! I discovered that his name was Kris Vallotton, and he was not only the overseer of the school, but also its founder. My family and I eventually moved to Redding, and Kris has become a spiritual father and prophetic voice in our lives.

This is the power of dreams. Our sleeping hours can actually be the most sacred part of the day. It is a time when our bodies are at rest, there are no distractions, and our spirits can receive from the Lord. If you are currently experiencing dreams you know are not from God, I break them off of you right now in Jesus' name! I declare your night season now redeemed for the Lord, and I release you to have peaceful rest and heavenly dreams. May you hear what God is saying through your dreams.

Steward what the Lord gives you in your sleep. You might want to keep a dream journal and pray over the things that are deposited into your spirit during the night. Good resources exist in the church for understanding dreams and their interpretations. Seek out such resources and get equipped to grow in the understanding of how God speaks to you through dreams.[12]

Glimpses

The Lord will often speak to us in pictures. When prophesying to others, we will commonly receive an image rather than a specific word. God loves to communicate in creative

12 John Paul Jackson is a recognized authority in this area. His website is www.streams-ministries.com.

ways. It is our job to learn how to discern what the Lord is saying through pictures. As we become more experienced in the prophetic, we will improve in our ability to interpret what we see. Symbolism, metaphors, and even clever word plays are all part of the Spirit's language.

For example, one woman was trying to get a prophetic word for her friend and "saw" a picture of God taking two dull dimes from her hand and replacing them with two shiny dimes. When the woman asked the Holy Spirit for an interpretation she heard, "I am changing your friend's pair of dimes (paradigms)."

Visions

God declared, "When a prophet of the LORD is among you, I reveal myself to him in visions, I speak to him in dreams" (Numbers 12:6). Visions have always been a means for God to communicate with people. Visions can either be internal or external, and they usually occur while awake. Internal visions are seen in the mind or spirit when the eyes are closed. External visions, also called open visions, are visible to the physical eyes. One notable instance was when a gentile centurion named Cornelius experienced a vision and encountered an angel in Acts 10:1-8. There are several other examples of visions in the New Testament.[13]

13 cf. Luke 1:22; 24:22-23; Acts 2:17; 9:10-12; 10:19-20; 18:9-11; 2 Corinthians 12:1-4. For further study on these types of revelations, check out Jim Goll's *The Seer.*

Trances

A trance is a semi-conscious state, seemingly between sleeping and waking, in which God communicates to people. Peter and Paul both experienced trances in which Jesus spoke to them.[14] These supernatural experiences occurred while they were praying, and they contained visual as well as audible revelation.

Being caught up in the Spirit

Paul described being caught up to paradise or the third heaven. The Greek word for this experience is *harpazō, from which we get the word rapture.*[15] *Paul wrote:*

> I know a man in Christ who fourteen years ago was *caught up* to the third heaven. Whether it was in the body or out of the body I do not know—God knows. And I know that this man—whether in the body or apart from the body I do not know, but God knows—was *caught up* to paradise and heard inexpressible things, things that no one is permitted to tell.
>
> —*2 Corinthians 12:2-4;* emphasis added

Angelic visitations

Angels are heavenly messengers commissioned by God to deliver special words to people. Although conveying

14 cf. Acts 10:10; 22:17

15 Strong's Lexicon G726, http://www.blueletterbible.org/lang/lexicon/lexicon.cfm?Strongs=G726&t=KJV

heavenly messages is not their only responsibility, angels are often employed to do so during crucial moments in history. They appeared to announce Jesus' conception,[16] birth,[17] and resurrection.[18] Most angelic visitations are fairly dramatic in Scripture, but the writer of Hebrews said people have encountered them without even knowing it.[19]

Visitations of the Lord

Though the Lord sits at the right hand of the Father, Jesus is still able to visit people on earth. Saul encountered Jesus on the road to Damascus.[20] Throughout history, and even today, the Lord visits people to strengthen, encourage, and enlighten. Hundreds of testimonies are coming out of the Middle East about Muslims experiencing visitations from Jesus and converting to Christianity because of them.

The Holy Spirit

Jesus made a remarkable statement to His disciples. He told them, "It is for your good that I am going away. Unless I go away, the Counselor will not come to you; but if I go, I will send him to you" (John 16:7).

The Prince of Peace, savior of the world, and lover of our souls told His disciples that it was actually to their benefit for Him to go away. For Jesus' absence to be beneficial, it follows that there must be something quite special about the Holy

16 Luke 1:35
17 Luke 2:9-11
18 Matthew 28:5-6
19 Hebrews 13:2
20 Acts 9

Spirit. Jesus went on to say that, "When he, the Spirit of truth, comes, he will guide you into all truth. He will not speak on his own; he will speak only what he hears, and he will tell you what is yet to come" (John 16:13).

The Holy Spirit demonstrates the heart of the prophetic by speaking what God is saying and declaring what is yet to come. Jesus also modeled this when he said, "So whatever I say is just what the Father has told me to say" (John 12:50). This is why Scripture teaches us that "the testimony of Jesus is the spirit of prophecy" (Rev. 19:10, NASB).

The Holy Spirit demonstrates the heart of the prophetic by speaking what God is saying and declaring what is yet to come.

If the Holy Spirit is our teacher, counselor, comforter, intercessor, and guide, it is important to develop a relationship with Him. Though He is still part of the Trinity, the Holy Spirit has a voice and personality distinct from those of Jesus and the Father. Spend time getting to know Him. The same Spirit that raised Jesus from the grave is living in us.[21] We don't have to go anywhere to hear from God. He is always with us. It is just a matter of cultivating a lifestyle of communication through intimate relationship.

Principle versus presence

For most of my Christian walk, I thought the highest ideal

21 Cf. Romans 8:11

was to live a principled life. I would study the Bible and learn principles to apply; however, I have discovered living solely by principles is not enough. Revelation must lead to a holy manifestation of God's presence. To remain only on the level of principle reduces our faith to religion, whereas abiding in the presence of God elevates us into a divine relationship.

Do whatever it takes to increase your communication with God. That communication includes not just growing in the prophetic, but also developing a healthy relationship with our Heavenly Father, our sweet Savior, and the Holy Spirit. If our Christian lives are just about applying good principles, we succumb to a refined, Old Testament covenant of law.

When communication is open and we learn what it means to be in His presence, then we live the life of love God always intended for His children. Let us draw closer to His heart and learn the many different ways the Lord speaks to us. Our intimacy with Him will become the foundation for our ability to prophesy.

CHAPTER 6

Understanding the Power of Words

You have probably heard the childhood rhyme that seeks to protect the heart and spirit of anyone who has ever been made fun of, belittled, or unfairly criticized:

> Sticks and stones may break my bones
> but words will never hurt me.

As many of us have realized, this is simply not true. Words *do* have the power to harm. Nearly all of us have been hurt (or have hurt others) by spoken words. In fact, the Bible says that *life* and *death* are in the power of the tongue. "Words kill, words give life; they're either poison or fruit—you choose" (Proverbs 18:21, MSG).

It is easy to observe the power words have in our relationships. We are naturally drawn to people who are positive and encouraging. They seem to nurture and uplift our spirits whenever they speak. Their words literally energize us. On the other hand, it is challenging, difficult, and even painful to be in the presence of negative and critical individuals. They are physically and emotionally draining. Life and death are truly in the power of the tongue.

Jesus is the Word

To better understand the nature of the spoken word, we have to go back to the beginning. John 1 teaches that Jesus was the Word, who was not only with God in the beginning, but *was* God.[1] Jesus was intimately connected with creation as the Word was spoken and life was formed. In Genesis, the Lord created by speaking. He said, "Let there be light," and there was light (Genesis 1:3).

A spiritual sound emanated from the mouth of God into the void, calling into existence something that previously did not exist. It is interesting to think God could have created our world through any means, but perhaps He chose to *speak* life in order to demonstrate the principle that the tongue has power to create life or death.

1 John 1:1

Humanity speaks the word

Part of what separates humanity from the rest of creation is our ability to speak words of life and death. This attribute of the *imago dei* (image of God) resides within every person.[2] People can create or destroy life by speaking. That is the basic idea behind blessings and curses. Jesus said, "Bless those who curse you, pray for those who mistreat you" (Luke 6:28).

How far are we supposed to take this principle of speaking life? People may find it difficult to believe humans possess a supernatural ability to create with their words; after all, you probably haven't heard of anyone saying, "Let there be a cheeseburger!" and a cheeseburger spontaneously appeared. However, Jesus repeatedly taught and challenged His disciples to believe they could do the impossible—as we will see in this next story.

The raw power of words

Jesus once saw a fig tree with no fruit on it, only leaves. In Matthew 21:19, he spoke directly to the fig tree and said, "May you never bear fruit again!" The tree withered immediately. The disciples were shocked. One would think they would have grown accustomed to miracles after witnessing so many of them over the previous few years, but the works of Jesus still inspired awe. The disciples asked:

> "How did the fig tree wither so quickly?" Jesus replied, "I tell you the truth, if you have faith and do not doubt, not only can you do what

2 Cf. Genesis 1:26

> was done to the fig tree, but also you can say to this mountain, 'Go, throw yourself into the sea,' and it will be done. If you believe, you will receive whatever you ask for in prayer."
>
> —Matthew 21:20-21

Many people believe Jesus is talking metaphorically here, but His words should be taken literally. Jesus had just demonstrated what could be done when speaking out in faith. The shriveled leaves of the fig tree testified to the power of Jesus' expressed words.

Jesus taught His disciples that they could also do the same thing if they had faith. That is worth repeating. Jesus said that His followers were able to speak to a fig tree and cause it to supernaturally wither. He challenged their thinking even further by promising an ostensibly greater impossibility: moving a mountain. The only stipulation for these things to occur was faith without doubt.

Could it be possible that our words have supernatural capabilities? Is the seed of the miraculous truly contained in our declarations? Our faith, obedience, and risk will determine whether we see the promises of Jesus manifested in our generation.

Ezekiel spoke words of life

Ezekiel, a prophet of the Lord, experienced the awesome power of prophecy when the Lord brought him to the valley of dry bones. Ezekiel recounted:

The hand of the LORD was on me, and he brought me out by the Spirit of the LORD and set me in the middle of a valley; it was full of bones. He led me back and forth among them, and I saw a great many bones on the floor of the valley, bones that were very dry. He asked me, "Son of man, can these bones live?"

I said, "Sovereign LORD, you alone know."

Then he said to me, "Prophesy to these bones and say to them, 'Dry bones, hear the word of the LORD! This is what the Sovereign LORD says to these bones: I will make breath enter you, and you will come to life. I will attach tendons to you and make flesh come upon you and cover you with skin; I will put breath in you, and you will come to life. Then you will know that I am the LORD.'"

So I prophesied as I was commanded. And as I was prophesying, there was a noise, a rattling sound, and the bones came together, bone to bone. I looked, and tendons and flesh appeared on them and skin covered them, but there was no breath in them.

Then he said to me, "Prophesy to the breath; prophesy, son of man, and say to it, 'This is what the Sovereign LORD says: Come, breath, from the four winds and breathe into these slain, that they may live.'" So I prophesied as he commanded me, and breath entered them; they came

> to life and stood up on their feet—a vast army.
>
> —Ezekiel 37:1-10

Again, God could have given life to the bones without Ezekiel. He is the one who created the bones. The Lord chose to use Ezekiel and partner with him in creating life. In obedience to the word of the Lord, Ezekiel addressed the dry bones and spoke words of life, and what happened? The bones obeyed! As Ezekiel was prophesying, the bones came together. Then tendons, muscles, and flesh covered them until a vast army stood before him. Ezekiel witnessed the immediate and dramatic power of his prophetic declarations through the creation of life. Jesus wants us to believe we have that same ability.

Our words have power

In case we might think Ezekiel's story is unique to a prophet of God, Jesus taught the same principle to His followers. Jesus and the disciples were in a boat when a great storm arose, threatening everyone on board. In the midst of the crashing waves and violent winds, Jesus slept in the stern. The disciples woke him, saying:

> "Teacher, don't you care if we drown?" Jesus got up, rebuked the wind and said to the waves, "Quiet! Be still!" The winds died down and everything became completely calm. He said to His disciples, "Why

are you so afraid? Do you still have no faith?"

—Mark 4:38-40

This may seem like an odd and harsh rebuke from Jesus. Some people think Jesus was upset because His disciples didn't trust His ability to protect them. I believe Jesus was pointing out the disciples' inability to grasp the fact that *they were capable of calming the storm through their own declarations!*

> I believe Jesus was pointing out the disciples' inability to grasp the fact that they were capable of calming the storm through their own declarations!

In the previous chapter, Jesus appointed His twelve apostles to preach, and He gave them authority to drive out demons.[3] How did the apostles preach and drive out demons? Through their words. If they had commanded a demon to come out of someone prior to their commissioning, they probably would have been laughed at or even beaten, but no deliverance would have occurred.

After Jesus gave them the authority, the apostles were empowered to carry out what they were called to do, and they saw people get healed, saved, and delivered. Jesus later sent out seventy-two more disciples to minister, and they returned with joy saying, "Lord, even the demons submit to

3 Cf. Mark 3:14

us in your name" (Luke 10:17).

A few chapters after Jesus calmed the storm, the disciples found themselves in a very similar situation, except this time they were without Jesus:

> Immediately Jesus made his disciples get into the boat and go on ahead of him to Bethsaida, while he dismissed the crowd. After leaving them, he went up on a mountainside to pray.
>
> Later that night, the boat was in the middle of the lake, and he was alone on land. He saw the disciples straining at the oars, because the wind was against them. Shortly before dawn he went out to them, walking on the lake. He was about to pass by them, but when they saw him walking on the lake, they thought he was a ghost. They cried out, because they all saw him and were terrified.
>
> Immediately he spoke to them and said, "Take courage! It is I. Don't be afraid." Then he climbed into the boat with them, and the wind died down. They were completely amazed, for they had not understood about the loaves; their hearts were hardened.
>
> —Mark 6:45-52

Right after the feeding of the five thousand, Jesus told His disciples to sail ahead of Him to Bethsaida. They were in a boat, straining at the oars because the wind blew so strongly.

They were probably filled with fear and tension because high waves were beating against the boat and threatening their lives. To make matters worse, the disciples saw a figure walking on the water next to them and thought it was a ghost. It turned out to be Jesus. He stepped into the boat and the wind died down immediately.

The Gospel writer Mark commented that these followers of Jesus were supposed to have learned something from their recent miracle experience of feeding five thousand people with five loaves of bread and two fish—something that would have helped them in their present situation. What was it? Mark said the disciples were "utterly amazed and they had not understood about the loaves because their hearts were hardened" (Mark 6:51-52). If you remember the story of the loaves and fishes, many people had followed Jesus to a remote place to spend time with him. It was late in the day, and the disciples told Jesus to send the people away to get something to eat. Jesus replied, "You get them something to eat" (Mark 6:37).

This was a command and not a suggestion. It is imperative to understand that if we are ever divinely commanded to do something, God will always give us the ability to fulfill what He asks of us. The disciples' immediate response was a carnal one. They exclaimed, "That would take eight months of a man's wages! Are we to go and spend that much on bread and give it to them to eat?"[4]

From their response, it sounds like the disciples actually had enough money to buy food, but were hesitant to use it for this purpose. Perhaps it was a test to see whether the disciples

4 Mark 6:37

would trust in their own resources or access the supernatural through faith.

Jesus then told them to find out what food was available. They found five loaves of bread and two fish. Jesus directed the disciples to ask the crowd to sit down in smaller groups. Everyone sat down in groups of hundreds and fifties. Taking the five loaves and the two fish, and looking up to heaven, Jesus gave thanks to God and divided them among the twelve disciples, presumably in twelve separate baskets.

Envision each disciple carrying a basket with broken bread pieces and fish in it. They then went out among the groups of people, handing out the food. The disciples must have realized something very quickly: the food in their baskets was not running out! It was actually multiplying while they were holding and distributing it. They were fulfilling Jesus' earlier command of giving the people something to eat. They all ate and were satisfied, and the disciples picked up twelve basketfuls of leftover bread and fish. The number of the men who had eaten was five thousand, and did not even include the women and children present.[5]

This has happened on several occasions in Africa with a modern missionary named Heidi Baker. Her group has distributed food that was woefully inadequate to feed the crowd, but God miraculously multiplied what they had so that it was enough.[6]

> After the feeding of the five thousand, Jesus commanded His disciples to get on a boat and sail ahead of Him to Bethsaida. Remember, Jesus' commands

5 Mark 6:36-44

6 Rolland & Heidi Baker, *Always Enough: God's Miraculous Provision Among the Poorest Children on Earth* (Grand Rapids, MI: Chosen, 2003)

> always come with the grace to complete them. "He saw the disciples straining at the oars, because the wind was against them. About the fourth watch of the night he went out to them, walking on the lake. He was about to pass by them . . ."
>
> —Matt. 14:24-25

Jesus watched the disciples struggling out on the water in the middle of the night. He decided to walk across the lake, intending to pass by the boat. Why wasn't Jesus planning to help His disciples? I don't think He just wanted to take a nice stroll on the sea. I believe He kept walking to test the disciples' faith in the face of adversity. When the disciples spotted Jesus on the water, they thought He was a ghost. At that point, Jesus reassured His fearful followers, got on the boat, and the winds calmed down. Again, Mark noted that they were completely amazed because they had not understood about the loaves; their hearts were hardened.[7]

The natural is transformed by the supernatural through what we believe and declare.

The lesson the disciples were supposed to learn from the feeding of the five thousand was that *they had the ability to do what their teacher did*. A good teacher empowers students to do what the teacher is doing. The miracle came through the disciples' own hands as they continually reached into their baskets to find the bread and fish were not

7 Mark 6:51-52

running out but multiplying. The natural is transformed by the supernatural through what we believe and declare. Jesus demonstrated to His disciples how to rebuke a storm, gave them an opportunity to experience a miracle through the feeding of the five thousand, and hoped to see His followers calm the winds through their own declarations.

If we maintain teachable and humble hearts, we will realize the lessons Jesus taught were not meant to amaze us but rather to instruct us in how to live supernatural lives. To those who are willing to embrace Jesus' words with faith, the doorway to the miraculous is open. Our words and declarations are powerful!

Stopping the rain in Mexico

A mission team from the United States was holding an outdoor rally in Tijuana, Mexico. Many people had gathered in anticipation, but the rainy weather threatened to dampen the entire event. One of the young students on the team boldly went up to the microphone and declared, "Jesus loves you! He is going to prove it right now by stopping the rain." He then proceeded to command the rain to stop. Immediately, the storm clouds cleared over the stage and the rain ceased falling. Everyone was amazed and it opened the door for many to encounter the Lord.[8]

This is not a new phenomenon in the history of the world. "Elijah was a human being, even as we are. He prayed earnestly that it would not rain, and it did not rain on the land for three and a half years. Again he prayed, and the heavens

8 Bill Johnson & Kris Vallotton, *The Supernatural Ways of Royalty*, (Shippensburg, PA: Destiny Image, 2006, 158)

gave rain, and the earth produced its crops" (James 5:17). If we, who are born into the kingdom of heaven, are greater than Elijah,[9] then we should aim to do even greater things than him. Elijah did not have the Holy Spirit dwelling within him. Believers under the new covenant do. Elijah is a model for what is possible when we speak out in faith and boldness. Our words are powerful when inspired by the Holy Spirit.

Words are Spirit and life

Jesus declared, "The words I have spoken to you—they are full of the Spirit and life" (John 6:63). This means when Jesus spoke, His audible voice came out of His mouth in spirit form, looking for open hearts in which to take root and produce life. The same Spirit that raised Jesus from the dead is resident within the heart of every believer.[10] When Christians speak prophetically, their words become Spirit and life, supernaturally able to change reality.

Another example of this phenomenon is found in the New Testament through the experience of healing prayer. Interestingly, Jesus never actually prayed to God for healing in others—He commanded it through His spoken word. His followers did the same. Whenever they spoke healing words, Spirit and life came from their mouths and manifested in the hearers' lives through supernatural restoration and deliverance.

Three stories in Matthew 8 demonstrate the power of words in the context of healing and deliverance.

In verses 1-4, a man with leprosy knelt before Jesus saying,

9 (cf. Matthew 11:11)

10 Cf. Romans 8:11

> "Lord, if you are willing, you can make me clean."
>
> Jesus reached out His hand and
> touched the man saying,
>
> "I am willing. Be clean!" and immediately the man was healed
>
> —Matthew 8:2-3)

Two simple spoken words transformed this man's life—from suffering and rejection—to joy and restoration.

In verses 5-13, a centurion approached Jesus to get help for his bedridden and paralyzed servant. Jesus offered to go to the centurion's house to heal the servant, but the Roman officer replied:

> Lord, I do not deserve to have you come under my roof. But **just say the word**, and my servant will be healed. For I myself am a man under authority, with soldiers under me. I tell this one, "Go," and he goes; and that one, "Come," and he comes. I say to my servant, "Do this," and he does it.
>
> —Matthew 8:8-9; emphasis added

Jesus was amazed at the man's faith and told him to go home because the man's servant would be healed, just as he believed he would be. Sure enough, the centurion's servant was healed at the exact moment Jesus spoke those words. [11]

Right after this, Jesus went to Peter's house, and demon-possessed people were brought to Him for healing. Verse 16 says Jesus "drove out the spirits *with a word* and healed all the sick" (emphasis added).

These three testimonies highlight the awesome power of the spoken word. Jesus taught His followers how to walk in this supernatural authority. Peter perfectly illustrated a student learning from the Master when he met the crippled beggar at the temple gate Beautiful. Making eye contact with the lame man, Peter said:

> Silver or gold I do not have, but what I do have I give you. In the name of Jesus Christ of Nazareth, walk! Taking him by the right hand, Peter helped him up, and instantly the man's feet and ankles became strong.
>
> —Acts 3:6-7

There is nothing wrong with silent prayer, but we are missing the power of the declared word when we do not release our prayers into the atmosphere.

11 Matthew 8:13

We are called to learn how to speak as Jesus spoke. Large portions of the church have moved away from voicing prayer to simply praying silently. In fact, many believers feel uncomfortable if they have to pray out loud. There is nothing wrong with silent prayer, but we are missing the power of the declared word when we do not release our prayers into the atmosphere. We must begin to believe and embrace the power living within us. May we walk in the authority given to us by our Lord Jesus Christ to prophesy redemption, healing, and reconciliation to a fallen world![12]

12 For more on the importance of our words, check out Steve Backlund's book *You're Crazy If You Don't Talk to Yourself*

CHAPTER 7
Stepping out in the Prophetic

All believers can be prophetic because the spirit of the living God dwells in their hearts. Although prophesying may be intimidating for many, it can actually be very easy. The first person you can prophesy over is yourself! In fact, you should make it a priority and a habit to prophesy and declare the plans of the Lord over yourself. The simplest way to do this is to prophesy the scriptural promises God has already spoken concerning you.

"The word of God is living and active" (Hebrews 4:12), and contains the power to accomplish what was divinely intended.[13] Interestingly, prophecy can breed prophecy. When we begin to declare or prophesy the truth of the gospel in our lives, we are positioned to hear more clearly from God and prophesy with greater power and anointing.

When we begin to declare or prophesy the truth of the gospel in our lives, we are positioned to hear more clearly from God and prophesy with greater power and anointing.

Here are some beginning declarations you can speak over your life to help you draw closer to Him. Get in the habit of activating your spirit and listening to your voice declaring God's truth each day. Let your words change circumstances by making declarations in faith.

Speak aloud these declarations inspired by Scripture:

- Nothing is impossible for God.[14]
- I can do all things through Christ who strengthens me.[15]
- The same Spirit who raised Jesus from the dead is living in me.[16]
- I can move mountains if I have faith and do not doubt.[17]

13 Isaiah 55:11
14 Luke 1:37
15 Philippians 4:13
16 Romans 8:11
17 Matthew 21:21

- I am a righteous person, and my prayers are powerful and effective.[18]
- I am a new creation; the old has gone, the new has come.[19]
- I have been crucified with Christ. My ego is no longer central. I am not driven to impress others or God, but I declare the reality that Christ lives in me.[20]
- I have the mind of Christ.[21]
- God is for me.[22]
- God loves me.[23]
- Nothing can separate me from the love of God.[24]
- God has good plans for my life.[25]
- I am seated in heavenly places with Christ.[26]
- Everything my Father has is mine.[27]

Prophecy has the ability to change circumstances. Even if you don't feel like some of these statements are actually true for your life, declare them with faith! Joel 3:1 teaches

18 James 5:16
19 2 Corinthians 5:17
20 Galatians 2:20
21 1 Corinthians 2:16
22 Romans 8:31
23 John 3:16, I John 4:9-10
24 Romans 8:38-39
25 Jeremiah 29:11
26 Ephesians 2:6
27 Luke 15:31

that those who are weak should say they are strong. This is not a psychological ploy nor just positive thinking; it is a divine command that reveals spiritual truth. Christians are sons and daughters of the King of Kings. This means we are royalty with a divine destiny and a future inheritance of the kingdom. God knows who we really are even when we don't.

In the human sense, prophetic declarations call things that are not as though they are.[28] From the Lord's eternal perspective, declarations call things as they really are. It is from this heavenly reality that we are to prophesy and make declarations. This is the heart of the Lord's Prayer: "Thy kingdom come, thy will be done, on earth as it is in heaven" (Matthew 6:10).

The citizens of heaven are strong, healthy, beautiful, vibrant, lovely, beloved, joyful, and part of a royal family. If you don't view yourself this way on earth, prophecy is a wonderful tool to align your present reality with your eternal one. Allow these declarations to become a natural part of your life. Saturate your soul and mind daily with the truth of Scripture. Let your ears listen to the living and active Word from your own tongue because faith comes through hearing the word of God.[29] Become proficient at prophesying over yourself, and you will not only strengthen your faith, but also develop your ability to speak life to others.

Always encourage

Prophecy is meant to strengthen, encourage, and comfort.[30]

28 cf. Romans 4:17

29 cf. Romans 10:17

30 1 Corinthians 14:3

Encouragement is part of the foundation of prophecy. Scripture teaches "Pleasant words are a honeycomb, sweet to the soul and healing to the bones" (Proverbs 16:24).

We should always be looking for opportunities to bless other people with prophecy. It is not difficult to find something to support or celebrate in another person. We are all made in the image of God, thus some aspect of the divine is demonstrated in each individual. Identify this aspect, highlight it, give thanks for it, and speak life to it for an even greater manifestation.

A quiet, elderly woman served faithfully every week in a church we attended together. She volunteered without much attention or fanfare. Her position of service was solitary and somewhat lonely among a sea of people.

One day, I talked with her and thanked her for her faithfulness and dependability (which are attributes of God). She was moved, and admitted to feeling overlooked to the point that she had considered ending her volunteer work with the ministry. I began to prophesy that she was a spiritual mother and that her presence brought comfort, peace, and security. I later found out this woman had been serving for many years, more than most of the other volunteers. Thankfully, changes were made to help her be more relationally connected with others as she served. She now has a renewed sense of joy and a greater purpose in ministering every week.

Most Christians are not familiar with Joseph the Levite from Cyprus, even though he is prominently showcased in the book of Acts. He is unfamiliar because he was called Barnabas, which means son of encouragement.[31] Joseph was

31 Acts 4:36

such a supporter and builder of people that they literally changed his name.

Are you known as an encourager? Encouragement is not flattery or sweet talk but rather genuine, heartfelt words of affirmation. Get in the habit of seeing people through a prophetic lens and encourage the divine within them. As we become more skilled at encouraging others, we position ourselves for greater breakthrough in the prophetic.

Activate your spiritual senses

Our bodies were designed to perceive life through five basic physical senses: taste, touch, sight, hearing, and smell. We touched upon this idea of a sixth sense when talking about impressions in chapter five. It has been theorized that this sixth sense transcends what we can know through the physical senses. Sometimes termed extrasensory perception or ESP, the mainstream understanding of this sense often gets labeled as psychic ability, gut instinct, hunches, or intuition. Although not much scientific support exists for such phenomena, I believe there is a sixth sense that unifies all of our physical senses—it is our spiritual sense: the ability to experience the supernatural.

All people were created in God's image and given a spirit. God is Spirit and we interact with Him through our spirits. Just as we can experience the physical universe through our physical bodies, our spirits may perceive the spiritual realm. Everybody has the potential for spiritual sensitivity; this sensitivity simply needs to be activated and developed. That is why Jesus frequently said, "Whoever has ears, let him hear."[32]

Prophecy is about utilizing our spiritual senses to perceive the spiritual realm in order to speak heavenly reality into the earthly realm. It is not only possible to *see* and *hear* God; many people have also testified to tasting, smelling, and touching things that were not of this world. We can train and develop our spiritual senses to become more attuned to the supernatural. Spend time with people and churches that are actively growing in the prophetic. Study the Scriptures and ask the Lord for an activation of your spirit. If expanding your spiritual sensitivity is truly your desire, take a moment to pray this simple prayer:

> Lord, I want to experience You with all of my senses.
>
> Let me taste and see how good You are.
> Let me hear Your voice calling my name.
> Let me smell Your sweet fragrance. Let me
> touch Your glory and feel Your embrace.
>
> Let me see Your face.
>
> Activate my spiritual sensitivity to know
> You more, in Jesus' name. Amen!

Love, compassion, honor

Everything we do, especially prophecy, should flow from a heart of love for God and people.[33] There is a reason why Paul

32 Matthew 11:15; 13:9

33 1 Corinthians 16:14

included perhaps the greatest passage on love in the middle of his discussion on spiritual gifts. God's gifts were never meant to be expressed without demonstrating His heart. Look again at Paul's words:

> If I speak in the tongues of men or of angels, but do not have love, I am only a resounding gong or a clanging cymbal. If I have the gift of prophecy and can fathom all mysteries and all knowledge, and if I have a faith that can move mountains, but do not have love, I am nothing. If I give all I possess to the poor and give over my body to hardship that I may boast, but do not have love, I gain nothing.
>
> —I Corinthians 13:1-3

Prophecy is an amazing way to strengthen and bless others, but it must be grounded in love. Jesus ministered from a heart of compassion and laid down His life for love. When we speak prophetic words to people, let us remember how much they are worth in God's eyes. We are to honor the glory the Lord has placed in each individual and call it forth.

Prophesying from pure motives

Proverbs 4:23 teaches, "Above all else, guard your heart, for everything you do flows from it". We have a responsibility to keep our hearts pure so that our prophecies may not be influenced by ulterior motives. Prophecy is not about control or manipulation but about freedom and encouragement. Even if we genuinely love the person we are prophesying over, we can sometimes prophesy what *we want* to see happen, or think *should* happen, in someone's life rather than declare what God is actually saying. It is important to discern the thoughts of our spirit from the thoughts of the Holy Spirit.

Don't worry about making mistakes

We have already discussed how fear should not deter us from being prophetic; however, many people genuinely worry about giving a bad prophecy. As a beginner, you are almost expected to make mistakes. Even the most seasoned prophets are not 100 percent accurate all of the time. It is unrealistic to think that mastery will come in your first attempts at any endeavor, let alone prophesying. You have permission to be wrong. Just be sure to learn from your mistakes to avoid making them again.

> God's gifts were never meant to be expressed without demonstrating His heart.

Seek accountability and oversight when stepping out in the prophetic. Paul said, "Two or three prophets should speak, and the others should weigh carefully what is said" (1 Corinthians 14:29). Find a mature believer to observe your prophecies, or record them so that you can receive feedback.

The person receiving the prophetic word also has a responsibility to judge what is said and has a choice as to whether to accept it or not. We should prophesy boldly, yet wisely.

The door to prophecy is open for all believers to enter. It is not an entrance to fear but rather a gateway to heavenly blessing, grace, and encouragement. The Father desires His children to step into the realm of the prophetic and to learn how to speak Holy Spirit-inspired words of life. He is waiting for you. Are you ready for the adventure?

CHAPTER 8
Giving a Prophetic Word

Now that you have a biblical foundation and mandate for the prophetic ministry and have been stepping out and prophesying over yourself, it is time for you to prophesy to others. There are four basic components of prophetic words: revelation, interpretation, application, and delivery.

Ask the Holy Spirit

The first step in giving a prophecy is "hearing" it. Prophetic revelation occurs when the Lord reveals something for you to share with another person or group. The Lord is always speaking life and destiny over people; we just need to be sensitive to hear what he is saying. Simply ask the Holy Spirit what He is saying over an individual's life. Remember, New Testament prophecy is meant to strengthen, encourage, and comfort. If what you are hearing doesn't fall into any of those categories, ask again.

> The Lord is always speaking life and destiny over people; we just need to be sensitive to hear what he is saying.

I remember after a church service, the leader invited anyone interested in receiving a prophetic word to come forward to the ministry team. I was on the ministry team, but I had never prophesied over someone I had not chosen beforehand. Usually, leaders would give the ministry team an opportunity to survey the crowd in order to get a prophetic word for an individual person. I was a bit nervous because a man I had never met before approached me and said,

"Do you have a word for me?" I replied, "No, but I will get one!"

It took a couple of minutes of awkward silence before I received and eventually shared a word, for which the man was grateful. I had to push past the fear and worry of trying to get a prophecy and focus, instead, on the Father's heart for His son standing before me. When we realize God's desire is to lavish love on His children through prophecy, the pressure of performance is released because we can rest in simply sharing His heart.

The most common question I ask the Holy Spirit when prophesying over someone is, "What are you saying about this person?" I then focus my spirit to hear, see, or sense whatever the Lord is communicating. You do not need to do a three-day fast or have an all-night prayer meeting in order to receive a prophetic word. In fact, it is not even necessary to close your eyes to hear from the Lord. These things may help, but they are not a prerequisite for revelation. The Father desires to have His children speak words of life, hope, and destiny to one another. He wants you to prophesy, so He is eager to share revelation. Just ask and then wait until you receive a divine word.

Prophetic exercise

One simple way to practice getting a prophetic word is to spend time listening to the Lord about someone you trust and then writing down what you hear. When you are done, you can go to that individual and share what you wrote. This is a safe, non-threatening way to develop your ability and confidence to receive prophetic revelation, while also providing an opportunity for the recipient to give you honest and constructive feedback. Ideally, we should get to a point where we don't need to be alone with God in order to get a prophecy. Our goal is to prophesy, at any moment to any person, by turning our hearts to the Lord and listening to what the Spirit is saying.

As we mature in prophecy, we will grow more skilled at receiving prophetic words. We can cultivate our relationship with the Lord and get accustomed to the different ways He communicates with us. When we maintain a constant state of connection and intimacy with the Father, revelation will flow freely and become even more detailed. He loves to have conversations with us!

Interpret

The prophetic revelation we receive may not always be straightforward or clear. It might come in the form of an image, a memory, a phrase, or even a physical sensation. Once we have a revelation, our next step is interpretation. We want to provide the correct meaning or message of the prophetic word so that we communicate what the Lord is saying. God often gives us pictures or cryptic messages when we prophesy over others, and it is our job to interpret what these mean. Knowing that the Father loves to play with His children, we should view interpretation as a fun game, not a burden. He is the author of creativity. Symbols, numbers, word plays, and even sensations are often part of prophetic revelation.

One time a man saw the Holy Spirit give someone a hat with a feather on top of it. He did not know what it meant, but he felt a gentle breeze blow and the feather moved. Immediately the Holy Spirit said, *"It is so this person can always tell which way the wind is blowing"*.[34]

If our prophetic revelation is not completely clear, our first response should be to ask the Holy Spirit for greater understanding. If we do not receive further clarification, then we can simply communicate exactly what He did give us. It is

34 cf. John 3:8

not necessary to guess or force an interpretation. Often the prophetic word is clear and meaningful to the hearer. Even if it is not, that person can meditate on the word and ask God for clarification. The Lord sometimes gives us a partial word in order to entice us to draw closer to Him. Any time we receive a word that we don't fully understand, we can think of it as a divine invitation for deeper intimacy.

Give a good report

Developing our ability to interpret revelation is largely dependent upon our prophetic lens. Our perceptions are influenced by many factors such as our beliefs, dispositions, and levels of faith. If we are pessimistic or cynical, such attitudes will probably skew how we interpret the words we receive.

When Moses sent twelve spies to scope out the Promised Land, ten of them returned with a negative report.[35] Only Joshua and Caleb gave a favorable report. All the spies witnessed the same thing, but most of them interpreted what they saw through a faulty lens. Joshua and Caleb coupled their experience with faith to open the doorway for the Israelites to fulfill their prophetic destiny and enter the Promised Land. Just like these two courageous men, we have a responsibility to maintain a healthy perspective on our revelations and provide a good report/interpretation to others.

Once, while I was prophesying over a man, I saw a picture of storm clouds over his head. I sensed things had not been going well in his life. Rather than immediately share what I was seeing, I waited for the picture to unfold, and soon the

35 Numbers 13

dark clouds began to part. The sun began to break through, providing light and warmth upon a vast field where flowers started blooming. I could have stopped listening or could have focused on the revelation of storm clouds, but God's message was not negative. I believe He wanted to communicate hope and encouragement to this man by showing him an approaching season of growth and harvest. This testimony illustrates the need to see things from the Father's perspective. He is a good God, in a good mood! This does not mean we sugarcoat our prophecies to delight the hearer, but rather we embrace our Daddy's heart of faith, hope, and love when we interpret His revelation.

Application

Many preachers learn that it is not enough to preach a sermon consisting of only theological principles and concepts. People will be more impacted by a message when it includes practical applications they can use in their daily lives. The same holds true for prophecy.

We may receive a divinely inspired word with an accurate interpretation, but if the hearer does not apply the prophetic revelation properly, it will not produce much fruit. Application is primarily the responsibility of the person receiving the prophecy. Sometimes, God will include insight for applying the word, but this is not usually the case. We can encourage the hearer to sincerely pray over the word, meditate on it, and discuss it with the Lord and other trusted leaders so that the word may be properly applied. People have a choice in terms of how they will respond to a prophecy.

Unless you are a recognized prophet, it is probably best not to give directional words to the equivalent of: "You should do this," or "You must do that." It is sometimes tempting to add personal thoughts or advice to a prophecy. If the Lord does not give you an application, just share the revelation. Allow the hearer an opportunity to spend time with the Father for wisdom in how to respond to the word.

Delivery

How we prophesy is almost as important as *what* we prophesy. Our tone, demeanor, and volume are helpful to consider when giving a prophetic word. When we understand that prophetic words are gifts God gives us to present to His children, we will be motivated to deliver those gifts in the best way possible.

When people genuinely care about the presents they give to others, they will take the time to carefully wrap them in nice paper, tie on ribbons, attach cards with thoughtful messages, and personally deliver them with a smile. We can adopt the same attitude with prophetic words by being joyful messengers who communicate God's words through respect, love, gentleness, and honor. Practically, this means we can speak clearly and loudly enough for the recipient to hear us without our shouting. We should use words and phrases that will be understood by the one receiving the prophecy.

Ideally, maintain eye contact when prophesying (although some prefer not to for concentration). I find that smiling is usually better than scowling when giving a prophetic word, especially since Paul says the kingdom of God is "righteousness, peace, and *joy* in the Holy Spirit" (Romans 14:17, emphasis added). When we deliver a special word to someone, it should match the nature of the kingdom.

Some people open or close their prophecies with a "Thus sayeth the Lord." Old Testament prophets commonly said the equivalent of that when declaring a message from God, but this phrase implies the prophecy is exactly what God is saying. Again, unless you are a respected prophet with a solid history in the prophetic, it is probably better to preface your prophecy with something like, "I feel like the Lord is saying . . ." This positions you in a place of humility and provides space for others to sincerely test the word without feeling they are going against God if they do not fully agree or resonate with your prophetic word.

Even though you may get a prophetic word for someone, you don't necessarily need to share it with that person. Sometimes, God shares things with us about other people so we can be better informed to pray or minister. Use wisdom and discernment when questioning whether or not to share a word.

> When we understand that prophetic words are gifts God gives us to present to His children, we will be motivated to deliver those gifts in the best way possible.

Timing is also very important. "Like apples of gold in settings of silver is a word spoken in right circumstances" (Proverbs 25:11, NASB). Consider the timing and setting of a prophetic word. Sometimes it is more appropriate to share a word in private than in public. If you receive a word meant for a group, share that word with the leader of the group first; he or she can then give you feedback and the approval to share it. We are called to honor those in authority and should submit prophecies to leaders before declaring a word to those they lead.

Take risks

When I was younger, I loved riding my Big Wheel (tricycle). My older brother and his friends always zoomed past me on their two-wheelers while I desperately tried to keep up. As I got taller, there came a time when I was finally ready to race with the big boys.

There was little risk riding the two-wheeler in the beginning because I had training wheels on it; but the day those round aids came off, I experienced a surge of fear. What if I fell? With patience, practice, and perseverance, I made it through those early stages of anxiety to master mobility on two wheels. I did fall, more than once, and I endured some scrapes and bruises; but I did not let those falls deter me from the joys of being able to ride a bicycle. In the same way, stepping out in the prophetic requires us to face our fears and take risks.

Scripture teaches that faith without action accompanying it is dead.[36] When it comes to prophetic ministry, our faith must be activated by taking the risk of giving prophetic words to people. We cannot let fear control us. Instead, we are to be bold and courageous because of the Holy Spirit.

36 James 2:17

Prophesying to strangers

A friend of mine, who was serving middle and high school students as a youth pastor, invited me to speak at a youth retreat. I had never met any of his students before, but my wife and I decided to take a step of faith and ask God for some prophetic words prior to the retreat. We prayed and asked God to speak to us about the students who would be attending. We each felt like we received names and specific words for certain students.

The first night of the retreat, I taught on the prophetic and then proceeded to share some of the words my wife and I had written on note cards earlier. My wife had received a word for a boy named Peter. I asked the large group if there were any Peters present. Three young men stood up. Not knowing which one of them the word was for, I simply read it to all three of them.

My wife had also heard the song "I'm Trading My Sorrows" by Darrell Evans.[37] She wrote on the card, "God wants to make a trade with you. If you give Him your sadness, He will give you joy in return, because God always trades up."

The next night, one of the Peters came up to me and thanked me for the prophetic word. He told me his father had passed away a few years previously. The retreat was near Christmas time, and Peter had been so sad during the holiday season that he had not even wanted to come. During the evening's worship, Peter was able to give God his sadness, and he could

37 Darrell Evans, "I'm Trading My Sorrows," *iWorship (Vol.1)*, Integrity's Hosanna! Music (1998)

literally feel God giving him joy in exchange. He exclaimed that he no longer felt sorrow about his father's death!

It took risk to share those prophetic words in public. Some of the names my wife and I thought we heard were even incorrect, but learning to hear from God is always worth the risk. It is our responsibility to learn from our mistakes and push past fear in order to grow in the prophetic. Prophecy can flow naturally from our spirits, no matter the circumstances. As we become more accustomed to pressing past our anxieties and discomfort, we will begin to develop greater confidence until prophecy becomes a lifestyle, not just a ministry event.

Negative words

If you sense you are getting a negative or discouraging word for someone, get some feedback before delivering the prophecy. Share the word with leaders, mentors, or even a prophet. Kris Vallotton, in his prophetic manual, states:

> The primary purpose of the gift of prophecy is not to *direct or correct* the body of Christ, but rather to ***encourage*** *the church*. We should never allow people who are ministering in the gift of prophecy to speak negatively into the lives of others. The *goal* of the gift of prophecy is to ***bring out the best in people!***
>
> We are to mine the gold that is within the dirt and find hidden treasures in people's lives. If we see negative things in someone's life we are

> ministering to, we are to ask the Holy Spirit to give us the answer to the problem we discern. Then we *prophesy the* ***answer****—not the problem*. That way, the person we are prophesying to will receive grace to solve his problem. (emphasis added)[38]

It doesn't require much of a prophetic gift to identify faults in other people. Close friends and family members are already pretty good at that. Our call is to see beyond the weaknesses, wounds, and shortcomings of others and, instead, to identify and encourage their divine identities and destinies.

What happens if you are wrong?

Sometimes we just get it wrong. I have delivered accurate words with inaccurate details. Prophetic precision is not the main goal when we give words to people. Our aim is to strengthen, encourage, and comfort others. Do not worry about prophesying perfectly because Scripture says "we know in part and we prophesy in part, but when perfection comes, the imperfect disappears" (1 Corinthians 13:9-10).

Conversely, Jesus teaches that we are to be as perfect as our heavenly Father.[39] It is a delicate balance to aim for perfection and continually strive to grow in the prophetic while recognizing that we may not always prophesy 100 percent accurately. If you share an inaccurate word, simply take responsibility for your mistake.

From a place of humility, acknowledge your error, ask for

38 Vallotton, 20.

39 Matthew 5:48

forgiveness, and seek restoration from the other party. It is best to avoid being defensive and making excuses. Learn from your mistakes. Ask the Lord how and why you got the word wrong, and ask Him how to improve. Seek out prophets or other leaders, ask them for feedback, and cultivate accountability so that you won't make the same mistake twice. You will build more credibility when you acknowledge your mistakes as opposed to denying them.

> Our call is to see beyond the weaknesses, wounds, and shortcomings of others and, instead, to identify and encourage their divine identities and destinies.

Sometimes, in our desire to bless other people, we may prophesy what *we* want rather than what the Lord is actually communicating. One prophet shared a very personal story of prophesying over a couple who had a baby with a terminal condition. The man prophesied to these friends that God would heal the baby and the baby would live. The parents were very encouraged and had so much hope for their child, but not long after the prophecy, the baby died. Everyone was devastated and the prophet was crushed. He apologized to the family and realized he had prophesied what he had hoped would happen.

Love never fails

A prophet was ministering at a church one evening,

giving great words right and left. After the meeting the Lord told him, "Those were good words *you* gave tonight." Immediately, the prophet understood the prophecies he had declared were from himself and not from the Lord.

The man began to repent and cry out that he never wanted to prophesy apart from the Holy Spirit. This well-respected prophet felt awful, but the Lord gently reassured him, "Don't worry. I'll make sure your words come true."

This testimony encourages me because it teaches that prophecy is more than a ministry—it is an overflow of a love relationship with the Father. We do not prophesy simply out of obedience or duty but because we love God and people. Obviously, we should not prophesy our own words, but our Daddy is gracious and patient with us during our learning processes. He wants us to prophesy!

CHAPTER 9
Receiving a Prophetic Word

Our capacity to grow in the prophetic ministry depends largely upon our ability to properly receive prophetic words. We will be more effective in ministering prophetically when we develop a heart that can embrace the prophetic, and that heart is routinely nourished with prophetic words. Just as there are healthy ways to give prophetic words, there are also healthy ways to receive them.

Test the spirits

Not all prophetic words are from the Lord. It is our responsibility to discern the source of words. As mentioned previously, people can receive revelation from four main sources: the Holy Spirit, their own spirits, evil spirits, or angels. The Apostle John wrote about this in his first letter:

> Dear friends, do not believe every spirit, but test the spirits to see whether they are from God, because many false prophets have gone out into the world. This is how you can recognize the Spirit of God: Every spirit that acknowledges that Jesus Christ has come in the flesh is from God, but every spirit that does not acknowledge Jesus is not from God. This is the spirit of the antichrist, which you have heard is coming and even now is already in the world.
>
> —1 John 4:1-3

We will be more effective in ministering prophetically when we develop a heart that can embrace the prophetic, and that heart is routinely nourished with prophetic words.

Jesus also admonished His disciples, saying, "Watch out for false prophets. They come to you in sheep's clothing, but inwardly they are ferocious wolves" (Matthew 7:15). This is a serious warning, evidenced by the large and powerful cults that form when people listen to the wrong spirit. Jesus taught that we are able to recognize true prophets by their fruit. True prophets produce good fruit from their lives, while false prophets create bad fruit.

Paul listed the discerning of spirits as a spiritual gift.[40] This is an important grace to possess, not just for growing in the prophetic, but also for our general Christian walk. When we receive a word, we can determine whether or not it resonates with our spirit. This means our spirit bears witness, or is in agreement with, the prophecy. This is not always a surefire test to authenticate a word, but it is a good start.

Another way to confirm the spirit of a word is to ask other trusted believers for their feedback. What was spoken must also align with Scripture. If any part of the prophecy is contrary to the standards of the Bible, then we have reason to doubt its authenticity. Finally, we simply need to ask the Lord for wisdom and discernment. The Holy Spirit guides us into all truth and can help us determine whether something is right or not.

If you want to possess the gift of discerning of spirits, take a moment right now to ask your Father for it, or pray this simple prayer:

> Dear Papa God,
>
> I sincerely want to grow in the prophetic. Please give me the gift of discerning spirits and the wisdom to use it effectively. By faith, I receive it right now. Grant me the grace to always listen and

40 1 Corinthians 12:10

respond to the Holy Spirit. In Jesus' name, amen!

Jesus demonstrated the discerning of spirits gift with His disciples. The Samaritans opposed Jesus as He was about to enter Jerusalem. When James and John saw this they asked, "Lord, do you want us to call fire down from heaven to destroy them?' Jesus rebuked them and said, "You do not know what manner of spirit you are of. For the Son of Man did not come to destroy men's lives, but to save *them*" (Luke 9:51-56, NKJV; emphasis added).

The disciples wanted to bring death to the Samaritans by prophesying heavenly fire. Jesus discerned they were not listening to the Holy Spirit but perhaps an evil spirit or even their own spirits. New covenant prophecy is not meant for judgment and destruction but for reconciliation and salvation. It is interesting to note Jesus did not address the disciples' ability to call down fire from heaven, rather He addressed their motivation. It seems James and John could actually do what they proposed.

We have a responsibility to identify the spirit behind a person's prophetic word. If it is not from the Lord, our job is to reject the prophecy. In some cases, God may even have us correct others who are listening to false spirits and guide them to the Holy Spirit. When we discern a prophecy is divinely inspired then we are free to move on to the next step of receiving a prophetic word—testing the word.

Test the word

It is possible to receive a prophetic word from God but communicate it incorrectly. Although people can listen to the right spirit, they do not always hear perfectly, and can even add to or take away things from a word. Just because someone gives us a divine revelation does not mean that it will always be 100 percent accurate. We are responsible to judge all aspects of the prophecy, even if we discern it is from the Holy Spirit.

God gives us freedom to receive or reject prophetic words. Ideally, we should receive everything that is from the Lord and reject anything that is not. If we discern a prophecy spoken over us is accurate, originates from the Holy Spirit, aligns with Scripture, and resonates with our spirit, then we may choose to receive it with faith and steward the word until it is fully manifest in our lives. We can respond to the person giving us such a prophecy by simply saying, "Thank you, I receive that word."

This acknowledges and validates the other individual as we declare acceptance. If the prophetic word does not meet the conditions stated above, we can still respectfully thank the individual, but in our mind and spirit reject the word.

As you become more accustomed to giving and receiving prophetic words, your ability to discern spirits and the accuracy of revelation will sharpen. Stay connected to the Holy Spirit and maintain accountability with other prophetic leaders as you progress. Proper discernment will open the door for prophecy to take root in your life and produce an abundant harvest.

Tilling the soil of our hearts

Jesus shared a fascinating parable with the large crowds gathering around him:

> A farmer went out to sow his seed. As he was scattering the seed, some fell along the path, and the birds came and ate it up. Some fell on rocky places, where it did not have much soil. It sprang up quickly, because the soil was shallow. But when the sun came up, the plants were scorched, and they withered because they had no root. Other seed fell among thorns, which grew up and choked the plants. Still other seed fell on good soil, where it produced a crop—a hundred, sixty or thirty times what was sown. Whoever has ears, let them hear.
>
> —Matthew 13:3-9

I used to think this parable contrasted believers and unbelievers. I understood believers to be the ones with good soil who produced a good crop and unbelievers as those who, for various reasons, did not produce anything. The Holy Spirit taught me believers also have the potential to receive a word from the Lord and not understand it, to let hardship deter them, or to allow the worries of life and wealth hinder them from obedience.

Therefore, it is the responsibility of every Christian to make sure his/her heart has good soil so that when God sows a word into it, it will produce a good harvest. Jesus even designated different amounts of return on His words: 30, 60, and 100 times what was sown. The variation in return is largely dependent on our ability to receive each word and cultivate it properly.

Mary and Zechariah

Luke illustrates hearts having differing qualities of soil. Mary and Zechariah each received a similar divine word but responded very differently.

Gabriel, an angel of the Lord, first appeared to Zechariah saying that he and his wife would have a son (John the Baptist):

> Do not be afraid, Zechariah; your prayer has been heard. Your wife Elizabeth will bear you a son, and you are to call him John. He will be a joy and delight to you, and many will rejoice because of his birth, for he will be great in the sight of the Lord. He is never to take wine or other fermented drink, and he will be filled with the Holy Spirit even before he is born. He will bring back many of the people of Israel to the Lord their God. And he will go on before the Lord, in the spirit and power of Elijah, to turn the hearts of the parents to their children and the disobedient to the wisdom of the righteous—to make ready a people prepared for the Lord.
>
> —Luke 1:13-17

Zechariah replied with uncertainty and doubt, asking, "How can I be sure of this? I am an old man and my wife is well along in years." The angel Gabriel responded by saying, "And now you will be silent and not able to speak until the day this happens because you did not believe my words, which will come true at their appointed time" (Luke 1:18-20).

> God is looking for people who will say what He is saying and do what He is doing.

This story illustrates the importance of faith when receiving a prophetic word. It is significant that Zechariah was unable to speak because of his unbelief. When we fail to receive the word of the Lord properly, we are hindered from declaring it! God is looking for people who will say what He is saying and do what He is doing. It requires trust, courage, and patience to embrace a prophetic word and believe it will come to pass.

The same angel who spoke to Zechariah was sent to Mary. He gave her an even more incredible message than he had given Zechariah:

> In the sixth month of Elizabeth's pregnancy, God sent the angel Gabriel to Nazareth, a town in Galilee, to a virgin pledged to be married to a man named Joseph, a descendant of David. The virgin's name was Mary.
>
> The angel went to her and said, "Greetings, you who are highly favored! The Lord is with you."

> Mary was greatly troubled at his words and wondered what kind of greeting this might be. But the angel said to her, "Do not be afraid, Mary; you have found favor with God. You will conceive and give birth to a son, and you are to call him Jesus. He will be great and will be called the Son of the Most High. The Lord God will give him the throne of his father David, and he will reign over Jacob's descendants forever; his kingdom will never end."
>
> "How will this be," Mary asked the angel, "since I am a virgin?"
>
> The angel answered, "The Holy Spirit will come on you, and the power of the Most High will overshadow you. So the holy one to be born will be called the Son of God. Even Elizabeth your relative is going to have a child in her old age, and she who was said to be unable to conceive is in her sixth month. For no word from God will ever fail."
>
> —Luke 1:26-37

The angel Gabriel not only brought a message of the Lord, he also prophesied to Mary when he said, "The Holy Spirit will come upon you, and the power of the Most High will overshadow you." Mary is a model for how to receive a prophetic word. She responded by saying, "I am the Lord's servant. May it be to me as you have said" (Luke 1:38).

In that holy moment, Mary chose not to doubt. Her ability to receive the angel's prophecy with humble faith opened the door for Jesus to be conceived in her womb and for her to become the mother of the Savior of the world.

After her angelic encounter, Mary hurried to see her relative Elizabeth in Judea. When Elizabeth heard Mary's greeting, her own baby (John the Baptist) leapt for joy in her womb. Elizabeth was filled with the Holy Spirit and exclaimed to Mary, "Blessed are you among women, and blessed is the fruit of your womb! *And blessed is she who believed that there would be a fulfillment of what had been spoken to her by the Lord*" (Luke 1:39-42, 45; emphasis added).

When we maintain a heart of good soil, we provide a place for the seed of God to take root and grow.

Most Christians have not had angelic visitations like Zechariah's and Mary's, but with any prophetic word we receive from the Lord, we have a choice of whether to respond with faith or doubt. When we maintain a heart of good soil, we provide a place for the seed of God to take root and grow. The Greek word for seed is *sperma*.[41] Mary demonstrated how to properly receive the seed of the Lord. She literally carried and nurtured the

41 Strong's Lexicon G4690, http://www.blueletterbible.org/lang/lexicon/lexicon.cfm?Strongs=G4690&t=KJV

word of God within her for nine months until she finally gave birth to the Word and was holding the fruit of the prophecy in her arms.

Mary potentially faced rejection, ostracism, and even death for being a young, unwed, pregnant, Jewish girl. Even though she did not fully understand the prophetic word or her remarkable circumstances, she trusted in God and did whatever she could to care for the Word. Can you picture Mary, sitting in a chair, rubbing her growing belly, and singing a song to this miracle baby? She may have been the first person on earth to praise the name of Jesus. She was probably reciting the angel's prophecy over and over, declaring to the fetus, "I love You, Jesus! You will be great and will be called the Son of the Most High. The Lord God will give You the throne of Your father David, and You will reign over the house of Jacob forever. Your kingdom will never end."

Unlike Zechariah, who could not speak, Mary's faith allowed her to prophesy the word of the Lord over and over. Luke 2 gives us further insight into how Mary received the prophetic word. After Jesus was born and the shepherds visited the manger, verse 19 says that, "Mary treasured up all these things and pondered them in her heart." She intentionally protected, cherished, processed, and nurtured what she heard. She gave the prophecy a home in her heart and allowed it to gestate until it was ready to be birthed. We can look to Mary's example when we receive and steward prophetic words.

Treasuring the prophetic

People tend to exhibit extreme measures of care and attention to the things they deem valuable. They will lock up jewelry in a safe, wash and wax a classic car until it shines, and prominently display a trophy or medal in a glass case. We should treasure our prophecies with even greater thought and consideration. What is our response to the prophecies spoken over us?

Jesus, the amazing miracle worker, prophesied we will do even greater things than He did because He was going to the Father.[42] What is your initial reaction to hearing this word? Many immediately reject it, not believing that this is even possible for humans. Others try to interpret and rationalize what exactly "greater works" might mean in order to justify a non-supernatural lifestyle.

God is looking for people like Mary—who will treasure, cherish, and cultivate His word and persevere until it becomes a reality. Though we may not fully understand how Jesus' prophecy will come about in our lives, we shall continue to declare it in faith.

Steward the word

Stewardship is properly caring for that which we are given. The term is often used in the context of finances. Though it is helpful to save, invest, and wisely manage our money, the spiritual realm operates with different standards of value. Prophecies are more valuable than earthly riches because they pertain to the eternal rather than temporal. Therefore,

42 John 14:12

we should take even greater care of the heavenly words spoken over us.

We are called to carefully steward the prophetic words we receive. We can write them down, memorize them, declare them, pray about them, and strategically position ourselves for the words to take root and produce fruit in our lives. True faith is coupled with action. If we receive a prophecy that says we will preach to multitudes, we can start by sharing the gospel to individuals around us or leading a small group.

Perhaps you were told you would write books that teach others about His goodness; try creating a blog or submitting articles for your church newsletter. Don't despise the day of small beginnings[43] but make an effort to enter into that word. Some people won't act because the vision seems too great. What these individuals don't realize is that destiny is always a process, a destination which requires a journey. By taking the first steps, you are that much closer to destiny's fulfillment in your life.

Honor the messenger

Jesus taught that if we receive a prophet in the name of a prophet, we will receive a prophet's reward.[44] A prophet's reward is the grace to see prophecy fulfilled in our lives. The reward can also be an impartation for greater spiritual sensitivity, or eyes to see and ears to hear. Receiving prophets means recognizing and honoring their authority and valuing what they declare. This

43 cf. Zechariah 4:10

44 Matthew 10:41

may seem like an easy task if we receive a prophetic word from a recognized prophet or respected Christian leader, but we will probably not receive most of our words from such established sources.

All believers are called to prophesy, so there is a good chance you will receive a prophetic word from someone who is not called as a prophet. The package or vessel through which your prophetic word comes may not always be conventional or attractive, but it can still be powerful. God likes to hide His word in unlikely places to keep us hungry, dependent, and humble. The Lord even used a donkey to speak to Balaam.[45]

Young children are being trained to prophesy at the church I used to attend, and many people have testified to the children's accuracy and detail. The motto was, "Children don't have a junior Holy Spirit." Some believers have difficulty receiving a prophetic word from children because of their age and lack of maturity. We are called to recognize the Spirit of God on the people around us and to honor those He has chosen as messengers of divine revelation. When we do, we will open the door for great blessings and increase in our lives.

Waiting on prophecies

The fruit of the Spirit includes patience, and patience is crucial when receiving prophecies. Throughout Scripture,

45 Numbers 22:30

prophecies required years and even generations to fulfill. Abram was prophesied to be the father of many nations but he waited a decade just to become a father of one son.[46] David was told he would be king, but that did not become a reality for fifteen more years.[47] Some people heard prophecies that did not come to pass within their lifetimes. Jesus said to His disciples, "Many prophets and righteous people longed to see what you see but did not see it, and to hear what you hear but did not hear it" (Matthew 13:7). Thankfully, those who have passed on are part of the cloud of witnesses and get heavenly front-row seats to watch how the grand story unfolds.

God's understanding of timing can be very different than ours. He is infinite, we are finite. We live in perhaps the fastest era of human history in regard to travel, information, work, communication, and advancement. With time-saving technologies increasing, our capacity to wait has diminished; waiting has become an inconvenience. Peter declared, "With the Lord a day is like a thousand years and a thousand years are like a day" (2 Peter 3:8).

A gifted accountant, after reading this verse, began to think of its financial implications. He prayed to God one night, asking,

> "God, if a thousand years is like a day to you,
> then is a million dollars like a penny?"
>
> God answered, "Yes it is, son."
>
> After thinking for another moment, the accountant

46 Genesis 17:5

47 Cf. II Samuel 5

asked, "God, may I have one of those pennies?"

God answered, "Of course—wait here a minute."

Do not get discouraged if your prophetic words don't come to pass right away. Often, the process of the word unfolding is just as important as the prophecy fulfilled. Celebrate the journey. Set goals and milestones related to your prophecies and invest in them. Write down the prophetic words you receive and continually declare them over yourself. Share your personal prophecies with friends and family and have them pray for their manifestation.

Just as in nature, the seeds of divine destiny often require a season to germinate, sprout, and bloom until they produce fruit; but rest assured, all of God's promises are yes and amen in Christ![48] When we properly steward prophetic words, our lives will become gardens of harvest for the good things God has promised for us.

48 2 Corinthians 1:20

CHAPTER 10

Prophecy outside the Box

Although prophecy is generally understood as speaking the words of the Lord, prophetic ministry is not limited to the spoken word. There are other ways we can communicate and release the love, power, and truth of God to the world around us. The Lord is the author of creativity. He is the Creator and He has crafted people with the ability to appreciate beauty, symbolism, mystery, and originality. Prophecy was never meant to be rigid or formulaic; it was intended to exhibit God's nature in and through what He has created. People are the expression of His creativity. Just as a significant percentage of human communication is nonverbal, so it is with the prophetic.

Several Old Testament prophets were called to enact somewhat strange and even offensive directions in order to convey a divine message.

☙ *Ezekiel lay on his left side for 390 days.*

"Then lie on your left side and put the sin of the people of Israel upon yourself. You are to bear their sin for the number of days you lie on your side. I have assigned you the same number of days as the years of their sin. So for 390 days you will bear the sin of the people of Israel"

—Ezekiel 4:4-5

☙ *Then on his right side for 40 days.*

"After you have finished this, lie down again, this time on your right side, and bear the sin of the people of Judah. I have assigned you 40 days, a day for each year"

—Ezekiel 4:6

☙ *Isaiah lived naked and barefoot for three years.*

Then the LORD said, "Just as my servant Isaiah has gone stripped and barefoot for three years, as a sign and portent against Egypt and Cush . . . "

—Isaiah 20:3

☙ *And Hosea married a prostitute.*

> When the LORD began to speak through Hosea, the LORD said to him, "Go, marry a promiscuous woman and have children with her, for like an adulterous wife this land is guilty of unfaithfulness to the LORD"
>
> —Hosea 1:2

Sometimes our actions speak louder than words. Though these prophets spoke or prophesied the word of the Lord, they also communicated what the Father was saying through physical actions. Although God may not be asking us to perform these types of extreme behaviors, we should be open to embracing and practicing unorthodox methods of prophecy. We still need to test the spirits and judge the fruit, but the church must not limit or reject the creative expression of prophetic ministry. In this next section, we will discuss various non-traditional forms of prophecy.

> Prophetic acts infuse earthly reality with heavenly power and/or foreshadow a greater spiritual reality.

Prophetic acts

Each of the Old Testament behaviors we just looked at was a prophetic act. A prophetic act is a physical action performed, at God's prompting, that supports His action in the spiritual realm; it is usually enacted to cause a change in the natural realm. Prophetic acts infuse earthly reality with heavenly power and/or foreshadow a greater spiritual reality.

The Scriptures are filled with many examples of God's people performing prophetic acts. When the Israelites were thirsty in their wanderings through the desert, God told Moses to strike the rock at Horeb with his staff:

> The LORD answered Moses, "Walk on ahead of the people. Take with you some of the elders of Israel and take in your hand the staff with which you struck the Nile, and go. I will stand there before you by the rock at Horeb. Strike the rock, and water will come out of it for the people to drink." So Moses did this in the sight of the elders of Israel.
>
> —Exodus 17:5-6

In the natural, Moses' action made no practical sense. What difference would hitting a rock with a wooden staff make for a bunch of thirsty people? But Moses obeyed the Lord's command and water came forth. This was probably not a little drinking fountain but a gushing river—enough to satisfy perhaps over a million people. This prophetic act not only released a miracle for the desperate Jewish people, it also symbolized and foreshadowed the ministry of Jesus. Jesus is our rock who was struck down and crucified for His thirsty people, so that streams of living water could flow from their hearts.

Another example of a prophetic act is found when God commanded Joshua and his army to march around the walled city of Jericho:

> Now Jericho was tightly shut up because of the Israelites. No one went out and no one came in. Then the LORD said to Joshua, 'See, I have delivered Jericho into your hands, along with its king and its fighting men. March around the city once with all the armed men. Do this for six days. Have seven priests carry trumpets of rams' horns in front of the ark. On the seventh day, march around the city seven times, with the priests blowing the trumpets. When you hear them sound a long blast on the trumpets, have all the people give a loud shout; then the wall of the city will collapse and the people will go up, every man straight in."
>
> —Joshua 6:1-5

Joshua obeyed God, and the Israelites conquered the city of Jericho. Again, this was not a rational plan of action. Rather than mounting an attack, they organized a parade. It was laughable as a war strategy, but because it came from the Lord it unleashed the awesome power of heaven on an earthly situation.

Hebrews 11:30 teaches that "by faith the walls of Jericho fell, after the people had marched around them for seven days". Prophetic acts require a change of thinking and great faith. I wonder if the people of Jericho threw spears or shot arrows at the Israelites as the army circled their city walls. The Jewish soldiers might have had difficulty understanding why they were just marching around and blowing horns while under attack. It just seemed foolish. There is no scientific or military explanation as to why their plan succeeded, but there is a spiritual one: Faithful obedience to God results in divine manifestations. Prophetic acts release the power of the Lord.

Prophetic acts were used in a myriad of ways throughout the Bible:

- Naaman was healed by washing himself in the Jordan seven times.[49]
- Moses held up his hands to help the Israelites defeat the Amalekites.[50]
- Agabus tied Paul up with a belt to foretell his persecution in Jerusalem.[51]
- Elijah threw his cloak around Elisha as a call into ministry.[52]
- Jehoash, King of Israel, was commanded to strike the ground with arrows as a sign for how many times he would defeat the Arameans.[53]
- Elisha healed the water with salt.[54]

49 2 Kings 5:9-10
50 Exodus 17:10-11
51 Acts 21:10-12
52 1 Kings 19:19-21
53 2 Kings 13:8-19
54 2 Kings 2:19-22

All of the rituals, sacrifices, and feasts of the Old Testament were also prophetic acts foreshadowing the new covenant in Christ. For example, the Passover feast is an old covenant tradition that prophetically symbolizes Jesus as the ultimate Passover lamb whose shed blood saves people from death.[55] The Feast of Tabernacles (or Booths) was a celebration of Israel's transition from slavery in Egypt to dwelling in tents before entering the Promise Land.[56] This festival was not only a commemoration of the exodus but also a prophecy that the Lord will one day make his tent or dwelling within the hearts of people.[57] The church continues to engage in the prophetic acts of baptism and communion, through which we identify with Christ's death and resurrection. I Corinthians 11:26 says, "Whenever you eat this bread and drink this cup, you proclaim the Lord's death until he comes".

Prophetic arts

The arts are humanity's way of expressing the beauty of God. When done prophetically, they also release His goodness, presence, and power. Prophetic art has almost no boundaries. When created for the glory of God and the blessing of people, our artistic declarations may take on virtually any form. I will just highlight three of the more common forms of creative expression.

55 Cf. I Corinthians 5:7
56 Cf. Leviticus 23:33-43
57 Cf John 1:14; Revelation 21:3

Prophetic Music

Music is a universal expression of creativity, passion, and communication. Though there are many different styles, prophetic pieces transcend genre. They have the ability to draw us closer to heaven and to experience the presence of God.

David's music helped Saul: "Whenever the spirit from God came on Saul, David would take up his lyre and play. Then relief would come to Saul; he would feel better, and the evil spirit would leave him" (1 Samuel 16:23). Divine grace and power were released through David's music that impacted the physical, emotional, and spiritual health of King Saul. Paul encourages us to literally sing to one another. He writes, "Instead, be filled with the Spirit, speaking to one another with psalms, hymns, and songs from the Spirit" (Ephesians 5:18-19). From earth, we can access the soundtrack of heaven to inspire and uplift people to encounter the kingdom.

Prophetic dance

Nearly all people groups in the world today engage in some sort of dance. God created us as physical beings with both the capacity for movement and an innate desire for it. Though individuals may vary in skill, dancing demonstrates the nature of the kingdom because heaven is a place of joy, celebration, and freedom.

It is rare to see people dance at funerals, but it is almost universal at weddings. Dancing is associated with victories and parties. When the Ark of the Covenant was brought to

Jerusalem, David danced with all his might while Israel celebrated with shouts and trumpets.[58] David foreshadowed the celebration that will occur when the people of God welcome the Lord's presence back into the Holy City. Prophetic dance shifts atmospheres, uplifts people, and ushers in God's presence. One time a few believers were ministering to a woman experiencing depression. Rather than praying, the leader of the small group felt they should dance around the woman in a circle. As they did, the woman felt her sadness leave and experienced a supernatural wave of joy until she was laughing and dancing with the group!

Prophetic visual arts

During my time at Bethel Church in Redding, California, I had the privilege of serving in the weekly Healing Rooms. People traveled from all over the world to this small city for a miraculous touch of God. Thousands have been healed. It is a joyful atmosphere, filled with musicians, dancers, and artists welcoming the presence of God and shifting the focus from sickness to the Healer.

One Saturday morning, a woman I'll call Janet (not her real name) came to seek a miracle for inoperable stage four cancer. The doctors had told her they could do nothing and predicted she would not have long to live. One of the artists in the Healing Rooms had painted a picture with the word HOPE on it. Janet stood in front of the painting. As she was staring at the picture, tears began to stream down her cheeks. No one was even praying for her at the time, but

58 2 Samuel 6:14-15

when someone asked if she was all right, Janet replied, "You don't understand. The doctors said that my case was hopeless. But my tunnel vision just left and I feel no more pain in my body!" She later went to the doctors and they found no trace of cancer!

A painting was instrumental in restoring health to a dying woman because it was divinely inspired and infused with prophetic power. Can you imagine a generation of prophetic artists creating works that bring joy, deliverance, freedom, and hope to those who view them? This is already taking place—people are partnering with God in creativity to release His supernatural power through the arts.

The prophetic ministry of Jesus

The life of Jesus is full of prophetic acts and symbolism:

- He was baptized by His cousin John in the Jordan River.[59]
- He was tempted in the desert for forty days while fasting.[60]
- He read from the scroll of Isaiah in the temple and then sat down.[61]
- He chose and discipled twelve apostles.[62]
- He turned water into wine at a wedding.[63]

59 Matthew 3:13
60 Mark 1:12-13
61 Luke 4:16-17
62 Luke 6:12-16
63 John 2:1-11

- He healed the sick, cleansed the lepers, and raised the dead.[64]
- He fed the multitudes supernaturally.[65]
- He was transfigured on a mountain with Moses and Elijah.[66]
- He rode into Jerusalem on a donkey.[67]
- He cleansed the temple with a whip of cords.[68]
- He was anointed at Bethany by a woman with an expensive jar of perfume.[69]
- He washed His disciples' feet and communed with them.[70]

Though we may not fully understand the significance of everything that happened during Jesus' life, it is important to recognize most of His works had deep meaning and purpose beyond how they appeared in the natural. Prophetic acts are meant to point us to spiritual realities.

Prophetic acts are meant to point us to spiritual realities.

64 Matthew 4:23-25
65 Mark 6:30-44
66 Matthew 17:1-3
67 John 12:14
68 John 2:15
69 Mark 14:3
70 John 13:5

The prophetic act of the crucifixion

The ultimate prophetic act was demonstrated when Jesus willingly died on the cross for the sins of the world. Nobody in Jesus' day seemed to understand the significance of Calvary when it happened; but in that holy moment of His crucifixion, Christ became sin and humanity was reconciled to God.

If we were to watch a replay of His suffering and death, we would see no evidence in the natural that any of this occurred. Our eyes would simply see a bloodied and beaten man nailed to a cross, painfully gasping through His last breaths of life; but in the spirit realm, sin was overcome, death was defeated, and authority was taken away from the enemy! Christ's death on that cross was a prophetic act that contained eternal implications for all of creation. History was forever changed through what Christ did.

Living prophetically

Prophecy is certainly not limited to the spoken word. In fact, it is not even only for people. We can partner with the Holy Spirit to minister prophetically to nature, businesses, governments, and entire nations. As the church becomes more aware of the spiritual realm, non-traditional forms of prophecy will increase. Christians will move from a position of pleading with the Lord for intervention to one of bold declarations and actions that release the power of God.

As our eyes and ears become more attuned to the reality that "our struggle is not against flesh and blood, but against the rulers, against the authorities, against the powers of this dark world and against the spiritual forces of evil in the heavenly realms" (Ephesians 6:12), we will become more focused, wise, and successful in defeating the powers of darkness. Paul writes, "For though we live in the world, we do not wage war as the world does. The weapons we fight with are not the weapons of the world. On the contrary, they have divine power to demolish strongholds" (2 Corinthians 10:3-4).

We can live prophetic lives. Everything we say, create, or do can declare the heart and message of the Father. Let us not limit ourselves to religious paradigms or ministry protocols, but let us partner with the Holy Spirit in bringing heaven to earth through new and exciting means. All things are possible. The earth is groaning for our prophetic potential to be realized. Be a world changer by prophesying kingdom destiny to everything and everyone around you.

Everything we say, create, or do can declare the heart and message of the Father.

"Whether you eat or drink or whatever you do, do it for the glory of God" (1 Corinthians 10:31).

CHAPTER 11
Growing in the Prophetic

Though this book has touched on some scriptural passages regarding prophecy, *Beginning in the Prophetic* is just an introduction. To expand in the realm of prophecy, it is essential to gain an understanding of prophecy's role from the beginning of time (Genesis) through the end of time (Revelation). The church must get a firm grasp on the Bible's teaching so that it may fulfill its prophetic destiny. There are still prophecies yet to be realized. It is exciting to think that our generation can be the one to fulfill prophecies spoken thousands of years ago. May we be like the Bereans, who examined the Scriptures daily to discover the truth and experience its transforming power![71]

Enroll in the School of the Spirit

The best way to grow in the prophetic is to spend time with the Holy Spirit and get trained by Him. The Holy Spirit lives within believers and guides them into all truth.[72] Ask Him for greater wisdom in the area of prophecy and meditate on the Scriptures related to prophecy. We have access to the source of all prophecy through the Holy Spirit. If we have questions, concerns, or confusion about the prophetic ministry, He is always available and willing to fellowship with us. Cultivating our relationship with Him will not only give us insight into the prophetic, it will actually help us prophesy with greater success. The more clearly we hear from the Holy Spirit, the more accurately we will prophesy. Allow Him to be your teacher!

We have access to the source of all prophecy through the Holy Spirit.

Connect with and honor recognized prophetic voices

As we mentioned in chapter nine, Jesus taught that "whoever welcomes a prophet as a prophet will receive a prophet's reward" (Matthew 10:41). We have a choice to honor the people God has raised up as prophets. Although we are warned of false prophets, we cannot let fear hinder us from

71 cf. Acts 17:11

72 cf. Romans 8:11; John 16:13

recognizing and honoring those with a genuine gift and call from the Lord.

It is still our responsibility to test spirits, discern character, and judge everything by Scripture, but it is also our duty to seek unity within the whole body of Christ. Paul gives us a beautiful illustration of this:

> God has placed the parts in the body, every one of them, just as he wanted them to be. If they were all one part, where would the body be? As it is, there are many parts, but one body.
>
> The eye cannot say to the hand, "I don't need you!" And the head cannot say to the feet, "I don't need you!" On the contrary, those parts of the body that seem to be weaker are indispensable, and the parts that we think are less honorable we treat with special honor.
>
> And the parts that are unpresentable are treated with special modesty, while our presentable parts need no special treatment. But God has put the body together, giving greater honor to the parts that lacked it, so that there should be no division in the body, but that its parts should have equal concern for each other. If one part suffers, every part suffers with it; if one part is honored, every part rejoices with it.
>
> —1 Corinthians 12:15-26

We desperately need prophetic voices to be heard. Many of today's prophets have paid a great price for following their calls and stepping out in their gifts. We would do well to connect with churches that operate in the prophetic or have an established prophet.[73] If we continue to remain only with believers who are like ourselves, it will be difficult to achieve the unity God desires for the church.

Get impartation

Jacob stole the blessing from his older brother, Esau, by tricking his blind father, Isaac. Apparently Esau was hairy as a goat, because Rebekah had to place goatskins on Jacob's hands and neck to fool Isaac into giving Jacob the blessing reserved for the firstborn son. Although Isaac was initially suspicious, he eventually released a blessing for Jacob. When Esau later went to see his father for the blessing, both of them were dismayed when they realized Jacob had deceived them. Isaac said to Esau, "Behold, I have made Jacob your master and all his relatives I have given to him as servants; and with grain and new wine I have sustained him. Now as for you then, what can I do, my son?" (Genesis 27:37).

Why couldn't Isaac simply have given the blessing back to Esau after he realized the deception? The key to understanding this story lies in the principle of impartation. When Isaac blessed Jacob—and in all likelihood laid hands on him—a spiritual transaction took place between father and son. Something was transferred to Jacob from Isaac's hand that could not be taken back. Later, Jacob would be the one laying hands on Joseph's children and releasing a blessing on them.[74]

Many Christians do not know much about this special

73 See the appendix for a list of prophets based in America

74 Genesis 48

principle of impartation, though it was common throughout Jewish history. God even instructed Moses to impart a blessing to Joshua. "Take Joshua son of Nun, a man in whom is the spirit, and lay your hand on him" (Numbers 27:18).

The writer of Hebrews listed impartation as a basic teaching of the faith. He taught:

> Therefore let us move beyond the elementary teachings about Christ and be taken forward to maturity, not laying again the foundation of repentance from acts that lead to death, and of faith in God, instruction about cleansing rites, **the laying on of hands**, the resurrection of the dead, and eternal judgment. And God permitting, we will do so.
>
> —Hebrews 6:1-3; emphasis added

Paul understood the importance of impartation in the life of the church; in fact, Christ ordained this practice of laying hands on another believer to pass along a spiritual blessing or gift. Jesus said we have freely received his gifts so we should freely give them away.[75] Paul wrote to the Romans, "I long to see you so that I may impart to you some spiritual gift to make you strong" (Romans 1:11). He also wrote to Timothy, "Do not neglect your gift, which was given you through prophecy when the body of elders laid their hands on you" (I Timothy 4:14).

I have a friend who is gifted in words of knowledge for

75 Matthew 10:8

healing—the special grace of supernaturally knowing if there is something physically wrong with another person. My friend has seen many healings when he uses this gift before praying for people. I asked him to impart his gift to me. Shortly after he prayed for me, I noticed a significant increase in my words of knowledge for healing. Since that time, I have been with individuals and large groups where I could sense certain conditions or health issues with greater accuracy.

Find people who are gifted in the prophetic, and have them lay hands on you and pray for an impartation of their gift. As you do this, activate what you receive by taking greater risks in prophesying to others. You will notice a significant increase in the quality, depth, and power of your words. I would also encourage you to impart what you have to other people. Everyone is at a different place in his prophetic journey, so share the gifts God has given you, too.

Practice, practice, practice

Just as with any other art or discipline, proficiency comes with practice. The more you prophesy to others, the better you will become at it. I remember being very unsure of myself when I first began giving prophetic words to people. I doubted my perceptions and the accuracy of my words. It was only after several months of prophesying that I started becoming more confident about what I was saying. A positive shift happened when I embraced the truth that God really does speak to us and give us revelation for others. Consistent practice helps to renew our minds, and it increases our faith to walk in higher levels of prophetic power and accuracy.

Challenge, train, and push yourself to prophesy over everyone you encounter. Grow your gift.

Create a prophetic culture

Growing in the prophetic is important for every believer, but it's not just a mission for individuals. Churches can create communities and environments that promote, teach, encourage, and practice prophecy. Our goal should be to raise up an entire generation that is able to accurately hear from the Lord and effectively minister in the prophetic. As Paul commands, we should eagerly desire the spiritual gifts—especially prophecy.

> Consistent practice helps to renew our minds, and it increases our faith to walk in higher levels of prophetic power and accuracy.

Developing the prophetic within people can change the entire culture of a congregation. A leader once said she loved listening to other people's prophecies because she could then treat others the way God sees them—and not necessarily as they appeared to be. A prophetic culture can transform the way people see and interact with others.

A church that is walking in the gift of prophecy will identify, encourage, and call forth the greatness in others rather than focus on faults or imperfections. Can you imagine an entire congregation speaking prophetic words that launch people into their destinies with supernatural power and grace? It is not only possible; it is already beginning to happen in churches throughout the world.

Establishing a structure that nurtures the prophetic

In the Old Testament, if a prophet gave a prophetic word that did not come to pass, the prophet would be stoned. Thankfully, we do not practice stoning anymore. We are no longer responsible to cast judgment upon those who prophesy, but rather we are called to judge the quality of their words. In the old covenant, the Spirit of the Lord would come upon people and they would prophesy. In the new covenant, the Holy Spirit dwells in our hearts so that we may all prophesy. Creating a culture that embraces and promotes the prophetic is paramount to producing a healthy church. But what might that look like?

> Our goal should be to raise up an entire generation that is able to accurately hear from the Lord and effectively minister in the prophetic.

To grow in the prophetic, you need a safe place to practice and the understanding that it is normal to make mistakes. Many people still adopt the old covenant standard of perfection when judging prophecy and prophetic words. Although these people may not throw rocks at others, they will discount, discourage, and reject anyone who does not prophesy with 100 percent accuracy. Such a reaction comes from believing the lie that only those with prophetic perfection are the ones who are called by God. A church that gives grace, oversight, and loving correction for mistakes opens the way for people to learn from their errors and take increased risks to grow. We need churches that make room for people to make mistakes in prophecy in order for the prophetic gift to flourish.

Teaching on the prophetic

God once declared that His people are "destroyed from lack of knowledge" (Hosea 4:6). It is our responsibility to learn the ways of prophecy and instruct others how to engage in it. The majority of the church must be reawakened to prophets and the prophetic ministry. Along with many other gifts of the Spirit, prophecy is regaining prominence in the advancement of God's kingdom. Jesus gave some to be prophets in order to "prepare God's people for works of service, so that the body of Christ may be built up until we all reach unity in the faith and in the knowledge of the Son of God and become mature, attaining to the whole measure of the fullness of Christ" (Ephesians 4:11-13). We will continue to need prophets and the prophetic ministry until the church fulfills her destiny.

Follow the ultimate model

Jesus is the truest example of what prophecy should look like. He declared, "I did not speak of my own accord, but the Father who sent me commanded me what to say and how to say it. I know that his command leads to eternal life. So whatever I say is just what the Father has told me to say" (John 12:49-50). He also said, "The Son can do nothing by himself; he can do only what he sees his Father doing, because whatever the Father does the Son also does" (John 5:19).

Jesus demonstrated the heart of prophecy in what he said and did. "The testimony of Jesus is the spirit of prophecy" (Revelation 19:10). God is calling His people to declare what He is saying over all of creation—words such as freedom, truth, justice, healing, wholeness, forgiveness, reconciliation, peace, righteousness, joy, faith, hope, and love. As we become more intimate with the Lord and more attuned to what He is saying, our prophetic potential will increase to the point where our words will move mountains and create worlds—just like Jesus' did. May we go forth and prophesy His kingdom until His will is done on earth as it is in heaven.

> "And you are heirs of the prophets and of the covenant God made with your fathers."
>
> —Acts 3:25

APPENDIX

Prophetic Resources from established and recognized prophets

Kris Vallotton

Kris is the Senior Associate Pastor of Bethel Church in Redding, CA. He and his wife Kathy are the Overseers of the School of Supernatural Ministry. They have four children and eight grandchildren.

Website: www.kvministries.com

Notable Books: *The Supernatural Ways of Royalty, Basic Training for the Prophetic Ministry, Heavy Rain*

James Goll

Dr. James W. Goll is the President of Encounters Network based in Franklin, TN. He was married to Michal Ann for 32 years before her passing in 2008. He has four adult children.

Website: www.encountersnetwork.com

Notable Books: *The Seer, Discovering the Seer in You, The Beginner's Guide to Hearing God, Dream Language*

Cindy Jacobs

Dr. Cindy Jacobs is a prophetic intercessor and founder of Generals International with her husband Mike. They reside in Texas and have two children and five grandchildren.

Website: www.mikeandcindyjacobs.com

Notable Books: *The Voice of God, Supernatural Life, The Power of Persistent Prayer*

Lou Engle

Lou is a senior leader at the International House of Prayer in Kansas City, MO. He is also the founder of TheCall solemn assemblies, a movement to pray and fast for revival. Lou and his wife, Therese, have been married for over 28 years and together they have five sons and two daughters.

Website: www.louengle.com

Notable Books: *Digging the Wells of Revival, The Call of the Elijah Revolution* (with James Goll), *A House that Contends*

Graham Cooke

Originally from the United Kingdom, Graham is currently part of the leadership team at The Mission Church in Vacaville, CA.

Website: www.grahamcooke.com

Notable Books: *Qualities of a Spiritual Warrior, Approaching the Heart of Prophecy, Prophetic Wisdom*

Shawn Bolz

Shawn is the director of Expression58, a church and missions based in the Los Angeles area. The Lord has used Shawn to minister to world leaders and influencers, especially in the arts/media field.

Website: www.expression58.org

Notable Books: *The Throne Room Company, Keys to Heaven's Economy, The Nonreligious Guide to Dating and Being Single*

Chuck Pierce

Dr. Charles "Chuck" Pierce is the President of Glory of Zion International Ministries in Corinth, TX. Chuck and his wife Pam live in Denton, TX and have six children.

Website: www.gloryofzion.org

Notable Books: *Reordering Your Day, Interpreting the Times, When God Speaks* (with Rebecca Wagner Sytsema)

Patricia King

Patricia is the co-founder of XPmedia.com and overseer of Christian Services Association. She is called to impact the media mountain and currently hosts a television show.

Website: www.xpministries.org

Notable Books: *Ears That Hear, The Light Belongs in the Darkness, Spiritual Revolution*

Larry Randolph

Larry and his wife Laura are based in Franklin, TN. They seek to equip the body of Christ to walk in the fullness of their prophetic destiny.

Website: www.larryrandolph.com

Notable Books: *User Friendly Prophecy, Spirit Talk, The Coming Shift*

Mike Bickle

Mike is the director of the International House of Prayer (IHOP) Missions Base in Kansas City, MO. He is also the founder of IHOP University which includes training in music, media, and the Bible.

Website: www.mikebickle.org

Notable Books: *The Pleasures of Loving God, Growing in the Prophetic, Passion for Jesus*

BURNING LAMP™
media & publishing
Website: www.burninglampmap.com
Facebook: facebook.com/burninglampmap
Twitter: @burninglampmap

CPSIA information can be obtained at www.ICGtesting.com
Printed in the USA
BVOW02s1822100615

404109BV00001B/1/P

9 781937 481049